Praise for

Women Are Creating the Glass Ceiling
and Have the Power to End It

"I love the candor in Nancy Parsons's *Women Are Creating the Glass Ceiling and Have the Power to End It*. It's time to start having real conversations about the years of ineffective measures to break the glass ceiling, and Nancy Parsons's data-driven approach to uncover its true root cause is the critical first step toward achieving actual change. Every executive team needs to read this book and rethink their current D&I initiatives. We simply can't have another 40 years at this rate of progress. Nancy's passionate, insightful words are igniting the right conversations and will help accelerate us to a place where the entire concept of the glass ceiling is obsolete."

—Angela Westbrock
VP, Global Operations, Lyft

"In an era when most of the expert commentary on women in leadership and the glass ceiling is simply based on anecdotal experiences and partisan agendas, Nancy Parsons's *Women Are Creating the Glass Ceiling and Have the Power to End It* provides refreshing insight. Her writings are data driven, backed by years of hard-hitting research and real-world corporate management, consulting, and executive coaching experience.

Unlike contemporary publications that achieve little more than simply documenting examples of the glass ceiling, *Women Are Creating the Glass Ceiling and Have the Power to End It* distills the root causes of the glass ceiling effect and provides solutions to work towards its demise. Women and men will find Nancy's work equally valuable and appropriately timed for today's current climate."

—Steven C. Agee, PhD
Dean and Professor of Economics,
Meinders School of Business (AACSB),
Oklahoma City University

"Nancy Parsons, in her latest book *Women Are Creating the Glass Ceiling and Have the Power to End It*, gave me fresh insights into why our progress to break through the glass ceiling has been glacially slow.

This is a critical time for women to step up and assume leadership positions—in corporations, boardrooms, and nonprofits. But unfortunately, fewer women leaders are filling these roles. Aside from external factors, Nancy points a finger at how women hold ourselves back and she's right; over the last 20 years, I've seen these principles at play when women are called upon to speak out.

It doesn't have to be this way. By applying Nancy's research and experience, I truly believe we can overcome these hurdles, stop being 'Worriers,' and achieve even the loftiest goals. How exciting!"

—Deborah Shames
Co-Founder, Eloqui
Author of *Out Front: How Women Can Become Engaging, Memorable, and Fearless Speakers*

"This book is so empowering, and made me realize I am not alone. 'Worrier' women are holding themselves back. We worriers are our worst critics and often take a rougher, longer, windier path to being effective leaders. Knowledge and self-reflection is powerful. Thank you, Nancy Parsons, for all the years of data, and writing this book to bring out the best in us!"

—Angela Byers
CEO, Byers Creative

"Nancy's insights into how women leaders can break through the glass ceiling are an indispensable resource for everyone. She manages to crystalize the obstacles women face in the workplace, yet also provides invaluable and powerful strategies to help overcome those challenges. Just as Nancy has built her reputation on helping women leaders succeed, this book will become the go-to resource for women who are looking to reach their full potential. It's a practical and well-thought-out guide. I highly recommend it!"

—Maya Hu-Chan
President, Global Leadership Associates

"Although we would like to believe that all barriers that hold women back from achieving the highest levels of leadership are systemic, that is not necessarily the case. In this follow-up to her seminal book, *Fresh Insights to End the Glass Ceiling,* Nancy Parsons provides additional compelling support—through research and experiences from women leaders and top executive leaders— that a 'Worrier' trait consistently interferes with success. This outcome may be frustrating for some of us to accept given how many highly talented women often do face systemic barriers, but it also provides a critical opportunity for women who have this tendency to recognize they may in fact have more power than they realize to influence their future success.

Changing organizational outcomes to improve leadership diversity is complicated and difficult. The more research-backed recommendations we have available to us, the better our ability to truly make a meaningful difference. And that's really what Nancy has consistently provided in this book: she describes the current systems-level interventions that are critical to create change, while providing new interventions to target the individual-level barriers that contribute to the problem.

Nancy also addresses some exceptionally difficult and sensitive topics around workplace discrimination, sexual harassment, and microaggressions, describing the tightrope we currently walk between identifying serious problematic behaviors and overlabeling situations to the point when it becomes counterproductive and even further victimizing. This is not an easy subject to address, but Nancy thoughtfully and directly approaches it through the lens of what works, what doesn't, and what the research supports. Finally, Nancy provides a wealth of valuable, practical recommendations from women leaders and leadership coaches, as well as from her own research, about what works in various situations. One way or another, you will learn a lot from this book."

—Mira Brancu, PhD
    Founder and CEO, Brancu & Associates, PLLC
    Author of *Psychology Today's A New Look at Women's Leadership*

"This book gets to the heart of women in leadership: how do women effectively lead and stand out with authenticity and confidence? Nancy Parsons describes risk factors that hold women back as leaders and provides solutions to unlock their power and personal strengths. I love the book because of its research-based approach, real-world strategies, and practicality."

—Simon Vetter
  CEO, Stand Out International
  Author of *Leading with Vision*

"I have known Nancy Parsons for several years and have both participated in her research and gained a great deal of insight from her findings. Nancy really understands what it is going to take for women to break the glass ceiling and come into our own as leaders. At Purse Power, we are all about taking positive, constructive, and effective action to reach our goals. Nancy provides us all with an invaluable road map for making the trip."

—Donna Miller, MBA, PCC
  Co-Founder and CEO, Purse Power, Inc.

"Nancy Parson's book serves as a powerful guide for all aspiring women by breaking down the myth of what might hold them back. Based on rigorous research and practical solutions, her work helps make the glass ceiling a thing of the past."

—Susan Diamond
  Vice President and Chief Learning Officer
  Women Presidents' Organization

WOMEN

ARE CREATING THE

GLASS CEILING

AND HAVE THE

POWER

TO END IT

WOMEN

ARE CREATING THE

GLASS CEILING

AND HAVE THE

POWER

TO END IT

Nancy E. Parsons

WSA PUBLISHING

PUBLISHING

Published by
WSA PUBLISHING
301 E 57th Street, 4th fl
New York, NY 10022

Manufactured in the United States of America, or in the United Kingdom when distributed elsewhere.

Parsons, Nancy
Women Are Creating the Glass Ceiling and Have the Power to End It
LCCN: 2019914901
ISBN: 978-1-948181-80-8
eBook: 978-1-948181-81-5

Cover design by: Divine Promise O. (Grafiz Designs)
Author photo by: Trish Taylor / Imaging Studios
Cover image: cracked window effect by dule964 / Adobe Stock
Interior design by: K. M. Weber, I Libri Book Design
Photo credits: shattered glass by Rost9 / Shutterstock

www.cdrassessmentgroup.com

DEDICATION

To Sonya, Reagan, Evelynn, and my future grand-daughters. This book is for you and all future women leaders, as well as the aspiring women seeking higher levels in leadership today.

Contents

Acknowledgments

There are many people who have contributed to this effort that I would like to sincerely thank. First and foremost, I want to thank Christine Klatt, who led this project while keeping all of our other key CDR business projects moving forward. I don't know how she does it. She is an inspiration to me in so many ways. Also, special thanks to Ivonne Perez Jones, Ana Jacome, and Danny Perez for all of your contributions.

Special thanks to Catherine Elliott Escobedo who is an outstanding editor and professional. We appreciate your patience and great work. Also, Kristen M. Weber did an amazing job on the book design and graphics, once again, on this second book. The editing, design, and graphics crew came through in terrific fashion, and I thank you all!

Special thanks to Bonnie Budzowski, my book coach/editor, who called it as she saw it, as she always does. Her feedback and guidance was not easy to take, but she was spot on. Based on her suggestions, I muscled through substantial rewrites that even delayed our publishing schedule; but, thankfully, the end product made it all worth it. Thank you, Bonnie!

A warm thank you goes to those exceptional "Worrier" women executives (Karen, Nicole, and Elaine) and the other six women leaders who bravely contributed to this book. Your stories are heartfelt and inspirational. You've all come up with clever and practical ways to manage or prevent your Worrier risk factor from holding you back and you are all heroes to aspiring women leaders whether they worry or not!

I am in awe of the top executive coaches who have contributed to this book. I have known most of them for many years; they are colleagues who are highly skilled in using CDR assessments in their coaching engagements. I send a warm thank you to Carolyn Maue,

Marianne Roy, Brian Epperson, PhD, Barbara Mintzer McMahon, Daniel Feldman, PhD, Lynne Pritchard, Patricia Wheeler, PhD, Rosa Algarrada, and Lynn Harrison PhD.

I would like to extend my deepest gratitude to Marta Williams, a globally recognized master executive coach and professor, and also to Stephen Adamson, Director of General Management and Leadership programs at IE Executive Education in Madrid, Spain, who allowed us to use the leadership CDR Assessment results of nearly 500 leaders and executives collected from their programs throughout Western Europe as part of this book.

A big thanks to my business partner, Kimberly Leveridge, PhD, who joined me in 1998 and took the chance to launch our firm, CDR Assessment Group, Inc., and develop our assessments, which remain unmatched to this day. Kim continues to serve as our Chief Research & Analytics Officer.

I want to thank my awesome husband, Bill. I adore him and am so lucky to have him in my life! While Bill has a very demanding and high-profile career himself as a chief medical officer in the energy sector, he's always supported my passion, energy, and the joy I gain from this work. He's toughed it out over lots of weekends when I've had to write, rewrite, and meet deadlines.

A shout out to my family who I love, and who all support me in a variety of ways. Angela, Katie, Jeff, Matthew, Lavanya, Andrew, and Rachel: hugs and thanks! Of course, my grandsons (not mentioned in the Dedication), Cole and Kiran, also get big hugs!

Lastly, I want to thank my sweet companion, Speedo, our American Water Spaniel who always kept my feet warm when I was writing.

Introduction

"When solving problems, dig at the roots
instead of just hacking at the leaves."

—Anthony J. D'Angelo

Ramping up existing efforts to advance women in leadership will not end the glass ceiling. When a solution does not work, doubling down on it never changes the outcome. Even many of today's experts and authors in diversity and women in leadership miss the mark on what to do; they are treating the symptoms and not the cause. The reason the glass ceiling remains firmly in place and holds so many women back is because its primary root cause is misunderstood.

Through our research at my assessment company, we found that the majority of women are holding themselves back, and this is the reason the glass ceiling is nearly impenetrable to this day. This is not intentional or a conscious choice by women. What holds most women back is their inherent personality risk factor as "Worriers." This risk factor causes women to become too cautious and more vigilant, to freeze, overanalyze, or retreat, and to go silent from fear they may not have the 100% correct response. They may seem invisible or lack confidence when facing tough situations, which is contrary to what we expect of leaders.

Women aren't the only ones with inherent personality risk factors. Everyone has them. Risk factors are ingrained, natural responses to stimuli that develop from infancy on up. They are part of who we are by the time we are adults. Risk factors could also be called our "ineffective coping responses" or "derailers." Risk factors are deep rooted, and most people have no clear idea of what their risks are because they go unchecked and unmeasured.

As the founder of CDR Assessment Group, Inc., a company specializing in scientifically validated assessments, we measure risks, as well as positive character traits and motivational needs, every day. In the CDR Risk Assessment, we measure a person's propensity for 11 risk factors:

- False Advocate
- Worrier
- Cynic
- Rule Breaker
- Perfectionist
- Egotist
- Pleaser
- Hyper-Moody
- Detached
- Upstager
- Eccentric

These risks run amok in every organization, and it's a problem. Some risks are more overtly damaging than others, but they all result in ineffective or inappropriate behaviors. They erode or undermine performance, trust, relationships, and communications.

Generally speaking, men's risk factors, unlike women's, propel them forward in today's organizations. We found that men leaders' key risks were as "Egotists," "Rule Breakers," and "Upstagers." These are aggressive behaviors that go against the tide. While these risk factors often manifest as intimidating or even disrespectful behaviors, aggressive behaviors in men are accepted as a common aspect of leadership. Men's risks cause them to oversell and become too pushy and overconfident; they do not lead men to freeze in fear as women do.

Risks tend to manifest when facing pressure, stress, adversity, conflict, or when the heat is on. How often is pressure or stress involved on the job or in leadership roles? I would say stress is part of the fabric of most organizations, particularly when someone is eager for career advancement. Since a person's risks show up regularly, women's Worrier behaviors undermine upward success.

I am writing this book to help women, executives, and all others who have interest in helping women succeed. I am also writing this book for those executives who want to markedly improve business performance results. Our efforts to help women rise to date have involved applying logic and what are typically sound principles to solutions, yet positive results continue to elude us. We need to abandon our standard approaches and dig deeper by using scientific measures that shine light on the source of the problem so that we can implement solutions that work.

As if ending the glass ceiling isn't a daunting enough endeavor, it is getting even messier. Since the #MeToo movement began in late 2017, and with the emotionally charged Kavanaugh hearings in 2018, many men have become rather fearful. They are pulling back from openly engaging with women and are pushing away from mentoring or providing individual support to their female employees. The research and solutions in this book alleviate the need for finger-pointing, shaming, or blaming, and will address real solutions.

Another stealth business issue tied to glass ceiling solutions is one that most consultants underplay. The stark reality is that for decades studies have consistently shown that leadership performance is 50% – 75% ineffective. This book makes the case that the best way to make significant strides in improving leadership performance is by promoting more women leaders. Even if men executives struggle dealing with the notion of the glass ceiling or gender issues, following the practical guidance and solutions in this book will help them significantly improve leader performance and bottom line business results.

I would be remiss not to recognize other exacerbating factors that contribute to the glass ceiling. These are serious matters like discrimination, the good ole' boy systems, sexual harassment, biased perceptions, microaggressions, inequitable promotional and succession planning systems, and the like. While these issues are important and must be dealt with effectively, they are not what keeps the glass ceiling so impenetrable. When women start neutralizing their own Worrier risk factor, they will have the power to transcend beyond these issues. A woman leader who no longer is held back by her own fear of failure is a woman in control of her executive destiny.

This book offers candid guidance to help women understand why it is essential to identify and manage their Worrier risk factor more productively so that it no longer impedes their success. It won't be easy, but it is certainly doable. Women will need training, coaching, mentoring, and executive support. This development and support, however, must change too. Objective measures are needed to identify each individual's risk factors (as well as their strengths and motivation) so that the development efforts can be based on their own true talent and needs. No more cookie-cutter or one-size-fits-all type training and development. No more leadership coaching that only scans the surface with 360° leader assessments or with the widely popular, lightweight inventories of the day. It is time to change our thinking and our actions.

Let's get started . . .

ONE

The Problem and the Power

*"One is always a long way from solving a problem
until one actually has the answer."*

—*Stephen W. Hawking*

When it comes to women in top leadership positions, the trends are dismal. In 2018, women actually lost ground. The number of women CEOs fell by 25%, leaving women holding a mere 24 or 4.8% of the top positions at Fortune 500 companies. Prior to this, in 2017, we saw a record high for women CEOs who held 32 seats or 6.4%.[1] As of June 2019, there was a rather sudden uptick to 33 women CEOs leading Fortune 500 companies, an all-time high of 6.6%; however, it was largely due to fallout from the #MeToo Movement and male CEOs being fired for ethical violations. In spite of this recent, anomalous upswing, only 11% of the top earners at the most profitable companies are currently women.[2] The glass ceiling remains stronger than ever.

This is true at a time when investments in women-in-leadership initiatives are at an all-time high—and studies consistently show that when more women serve in senior leadership roles, business performance improves. According to a Peterson Institute for Global Economics study,

> Companies with at least 30% female leaders—in senior management positions—experienced a 15% increase in profitability of more than 20,000 global companies from 91 countries.[3]

This is just one of the many studies showing similar results. So, even if we forget about the gender disparity for a moment and think about company performance and the bottom line, we would realize it makes business sense to promote more women.

Looking back in history, the US Pregnancy Discrimination Act went into effect in 1979, and, along with the earlier Civil Rights Act of 1964, the doors were *finally* wide open for women to be promoted based on their talent and performance. That was four decades ago, yet the numbers of women reaching the CEO or C-Suite level are dismal. Women's progress continues to be stalled and perhaps, one could argue, is sliding backwards.

Interestingly, every year since 1982, women have been surpassing men in the number of bachelor's degrees conferred. Since 2005, women have also received more master's and doctorate degrees.

With gender diversity initiatives in high gear, organizations are launching new women-in-leadership developmental and mentoring programs and are diligently tracking the progress of women's upward success. My firm's ongoing research reveals that while the intentions and investments are positive, today's solutions are not addressing the key problem. Using the same approaches will not produce different results. Here's a disturbing conclusion from my 2017 book, *Fresh Insights to END the Glass Ceiling*:

> *"If we stay on the same trajectory, it will take 400 years for women to reach just 50% of the CEO positions."*

Before you dismiss me as a doomsday prophet, note that McKinsey's study, Women in the Workplace 2018, shows a similar finding. This study reports that, at the current rate, we will only move forward 1% in the next 10 years.[4] If multiplied forward, it will take 450 years for women to attain 50% of the CEO positions.

In December 2018, the Global Gender Gap Report stated, "At the current rate of change, the economic gender parity remains 202 years off."[5] The results of this global gender study include all jobs in the private and public sector, while the 400- and 450-year estimates are based on women attaining CEO positions.

Clearly, whether it is 200 or 400 years, this wait time is unthinkable. To slide further backwards or to continue to not make significant progress is unacceptable and preventable.

So, with investments in developmental initiatives for women leaders at a record high and women consistently earning more college degrees and advanced degrees than men for decades, how is it that merely a few women make it to the top? Why are investments in training, development, and gender diversity not yielding better results? The answer is that these well-intentioned initiatives are missing the mark on *why* the glass ceiling really exists and what is really holding women back. They are not addressing the root cause of the problem. Consequently, the solutions are not sticking or facilitating the progress needed.

The Research

Our team at CDR Assessment Group, Inc. did not originally set out to study the glass ceiling. When Kimberly Leveridge, PhD, and I founded our firm in 1998, our vision was to *revolutionize* leadership. We knew leadership performance was not particularly effective back then, and we were excited to help leaders thrive.

CDR is a globally recognized assessment, leadership development, and talent management firm leading the way with cutting-edge tools, executive coaching, consulting, team development, research, custom leadership training, and CDR 3-D certification services. From executive coaching to employee selection, we provide services that wrap around all areas of human performance. Our unique tools and distinctive coaching services are designed with the foremost psychological insights and applied business know-how.

Developing highly talented leaders and teams requires accurate, concrete, and business-oriented information about each individual's differences—character, acumen, inherent risk factors, and motivational drivers. Our CDR 3-Dimensional Assessment Suite® provides unique insight into a leader's key strengths and development needs in the following areas: character assessment, drivers and rewards, and risk assessment.

The CDR Character Assessment measures personality traits with seven primary scales and 42 subscales. This tool identifies leader or professional acumen, vocational suitability or "best fit" roles, emotional intelligence, key strengths, noteworthy gaps, and more.

The Drivers & Rewards Assessment defines and measures 10 primary personal motivators and provides important information about job function and work environment fit. This assessment, in the aggregate, is a great tool for measuring the living culture and values of an organization.

The CDR Risk Assessment measures 11 inherent personality-based risks or ineffective coping strategies that can undermine effectiveness, damage relationships and communication, and lead to derailment. These risks tend to be revealed under stress, conflict, and pressure.

ILLUSTRATION 1
The CDR 3-Dimensional Assessment Suite®

These scientifically validated personality assessments and our work with clients allow us to perform ongoing cutting-edge research. I'll share more specifics of the dimensions of each assessment as the book unfolds.

CDR 3-D Assessment Suite Measures

Character	Risk Factors	Drivers & Rewards
Your strengths	*Your derailers*	*Your passions*
7 primary scales, 42 subscales	10 facets, 50 sub-facets	11 risk scalers, 8 derailers
• Adjustment	• Fame & Feedback	• False Advocate
• Leadership Energy	• Power & Competition	• Worrier
• Sociability	• Amusement & Hedonism	• Cynic
• Interpersonal Sensitivity	• Humanitarian Efforts	• Rule Breaker
• Prudence	• Moral Platform	• Perfectionist
• Inquisitive	• Companionship & Affiliation	• Egotist
• Learning Approach	• Safety & Security	• Pleaser
	• Business & Finance	• Hyper-Moody
	• Artistic Endeavors	• Detached
	• Scientific Reasoning	• Upstager
		• Eccentric

CDR

SOURCE: Nancy Parsons and Kimberly Leveridge, PhD, CDR Assessment Group, Inc., 1998.

In a particular research study a few years back, we were comparing our personality measures—the CDR Character Assessment and CDR Risk Assessment—to 360° performance data (from a random group of 137 women leaders and 126 men leaders from 35 companies in North America) when we stumbled upon an unexpected finding—*the root cause of the glass ceiling.*

In this study, there was nothing unusual about the CDR Character Assessment results: both men and women were shown to have strong leader capabilities and strengths; however, the inherent personality-based CDR Risk Assessment differences of men and women leaders were profound and unexpected. Once we had time to mentally process and review these stark differences in risks further, the impact was clear: Women had statistically significant higher risk scores as "Worriers" while men had high scores as "Upstagers," "Egotists," and "Rule Breakers."

After our initial research, something still seemed off to me as I thought about the women who had made it to the top. I knew from coaching these senior leaders over the years, and from what I recalled about their individual CDR data, that they did not fit the Worrier profile. This presented a question that led us to the next part of our research.

We looked at the aggregate risks of women who are top corporate executives and women who are CEOs. My hunch proved to be correct: both of the executive women groups' CDR Risk Assessment data aligned more with the men's group than with the women's group of mid-level leaders. These risk differences have been key to their ability to make it to the top without being held back by the Worrier traits. The women executives we studied were able to remain aggressive and push their views and positions regardless of conflict and stress. They did not shut down and go inside their heads when times were tough. Unfortunately, many more women, and most of those in the leadership pipeline, have Worrier traits.

In late 2018, we completed a third study of Western European women leaders, women executives, and men leaders, and the results were even more stark. This data was compiled from Executive Education Department at IE Business School (located in Madrid, Spain) program participants that included women and men leaders and executives. The women leader sample size was slightly larger with 145 women. Their average scores as Worriers were even higher at 75%. While our original North American women's group in our first study was at 63%, both were significantly higher than the respective men leader study groups. The 294 men leaders in the Western European study had lower scores as Worriers than their female counterparts. These men had slightly higher "Detached" scores but did not show the same risk trends as the North American men leaders. What was different was that the Western European women leaders' Worrier scores were markedly higher. The executive women's group in Western Europe (IE.edu) sample size was not large enough but showed the same trends that we saw in the executive and CEO women in North America in the second part of our study.

Recent Cultural Shifts Are Creating Fresh Tensions and Dynamics

While we've been discovering fresh insights into how differences in risk factors impact men's and women's potential for promotion, major cultural events and shifts in 2017 and 2018 are impacting both genders in the workplace. As a result of the #MeToo movement, which began to sweep through the media in 2017, dozens of significant and horrific cases of sexual harassment were exposed, many that had been hidden for decades. This has helped women to begin to stand strong against abuse in the workplace. This was long overdue, to say the least. Then in 2018, the emotional intensity surrounding the Dr. Christine Blasey Ford and Judge Brett Kavanaugh hearings added to the gender discussion and tension.

Unfortunately, we are now left with an ultrasensitive climate of fear, risk aversion, and pushback from men executives and leaders. Meanwhile, women are becoming angry, mistrustful, defensive, and fed up. I am afraid that rather than making the progress women in leadership so desperately need to end the glass ceiling, we are moving in the wrong direction. Fear and anger, rather than rational thought, are running high. The topic of gender in the workplace has become a tinderbox. According to a survey commissioned by a Lean In initiative (LeanIn.org is an initiative of the Sheryl Sandberg and Dave Goldberg Family Foundation), the number of male managers who are uncomfortable mentoring women has tripled since the #MeToo movement first started back in October 2017.[6]

For Sheryl Sandberg, Facebook COO and author of *Lean In*, these findings are something to worry about:

If men think that the way to address workplace sexual harassment is to avoid one-on-one time with female colleagues—
including meetings, coffee breaks, and all the interactions
that help us work together effectively—it will be a huge setback
for women.[7]

In the mid-1980s, when I was in HR leadership in the pipeline industry in Oklahoma and Texas, I routinely drove hundreds
of miles with my boss and/or other male counterparts. There were
no other women in key positions in the industry at the time. I had
many exceptional and developmental work experiences at the various field locations where I was needed. There was no fear of working
or traveling alone with a man. I wonder if this can happen today. For
most people, the best learning experiences are on the job. If we end
up holding women back from real-world experiences out of fear, this
stymies their developmental opportunities.

Currently, I have a millennial client who is a high-level leader
at a top technology development firm in Silicon Valley. He oversees
a department of more than 200 people, of whom most are engineers,
and about 50% are women. The diversity and inclusion team at the
company was impressed and wanted to interview him so he could
share what he was doing to onboard and promote so many women
into leadership roles. He declined the interview. He told me he was
not doing anything special. "All I am doing is hiring the best people,
giving them chances to grow, and holding them accountable, but that
may not be what the diversity team wants to hear," he said. The other
telling comment he made was, "I make sure at every meeting that I
call for the women leaders to speak up to give their input because
otherwise the men leaders on my team will take up all of the airtime."
What is concerning is that even those men leaders that are doing well
developing or promoting women on their teams are fearful. He also
mentioned he will now only meet with women in open lobby-type
spaces, never in an office alone. Other executives have told me similar
stories. Men are fearful, which damages working relationships and the
ability to build and foster trust.

Solutions with Good Intent Aren't Enough

Examples of common solutions deployed by organizations to help develop more women for leadership posts include the following:

- Assigning a mentor
- Creating opportunities for networking
- Engaging an internal or external leadership coach
- Funding an MBA or certification
- Providing assertiveness training
- Providing on-the-job experiences
- Providing training targeted at negotiating skills
- Sending to leadership training

According to the McKinsey 2018 study based on four years of data and insights from a range of experts, there are six actions recommended that companies take to make progress on gender diversity:

1. Get the basics right—targets, reporting, and accountability
2. Ensure that hiring and promotions are fair
3. Make senior leaders and managers champions of diversity
4. Foster an inclusive and respectful culture
5. Make the "Only" experience rare (this is where there is only one woman on a team or role)
6. Offer employees the flexibility to fit work into their lives[8]

These are all worthwhile, needed, and practical steps, but they are *not* the ultimate solution to ending the glass ceiling.

Women Have the Power

None of these solutions addresses the fact that women are holding themselves back. Women are actually taking themselves out of the running for upward progression. ***No one is doing it "to" them.*** Women are, in fact, creating the glass ceiling themselves because their Worrier risk factor behaviors are pulling them out of the running.

So, what can reverse the current backwards trends and accelerate the end of the glass ceiling? The good news is that women themselves *have the power* to reverse the trend—and to do it rapidly. Our research and extensive work in leadership development shows that women just need a different type of development to get them past the glass ceiling. It begins with self-awareness and taking responsibility for their own careers.

Equipped with a new crucial level of self-awareness, including identifying their own inherent risk factors (as well as specific strengths and motivational needs), individualized development, and support, women can ascend to the roles previously thought unreachable or unimaginable. Each woman's success is truly in her own hands. With a new deeper level of self-awareness and a commitment to overcome self-imposed barriers, the sky is the limit.

As individual women grow in self-awareness, all others in leadership positions need to do so as well. Women and men alike need to understand that all personality-based risks are actually ineffective coping responses. Thus, rewarding any of them is not productive. Organizations have historically promoted men despite their risk behaviors. Currently, perceptions of risk behaviors are out of whack and women are judged more harshly.

The solutions in this book are not about bashing men or falsely promoting women. The research findings and solutions detailed in this book lead us to identifying, developing, and promoting authentic talent—both women and men—with objective, scientifically valid measures. It is about changing norms that have led to fictitious and subjective systemic performance, leadership development, and talent management processes. To do so, incorporating science, objectivity, and solid practices is required. It is about accountability. It is about helping decision makers see talent much more clearly, and objectively, so they no longer accept and promote bad behaviors, particularly those risks more typical of men. Decision makers should, in fact, give all leader candidates a fair look.

Systemic change will take commitment from the top. The C-Suite and executives, mostly men at this point, must champion new approaches to assessing, developing, and promoting leaders—both women and men. The historical cookie-cutter, superficial approaches to these processes and decisions need to be tossed. We must add science and objectivity to end the gender-biased leadership selection, promotions, and succession planning results.

Despite the anxiety, chaos, and unsettled times, there is good news. There is a clear path to ending the glass ceiling that is a win-win for women, men, and the organizations they serve. The research in this book reveals this straightforward course.

TWO

A Brief History

*"The question isn't who is going to let me;
it's who is going to stop me?"*

—*Ayn Rand*

1964

As a six-year-old girl growing up in Norwood, PA, I was busy playing with Barbies when the Civil Rights Act of 1964 went into effect, which made it unlawful for employers to do the following:

> To fail or refuse to hire or to discharge any individual, or otherwise to discriminate against any individual with respect to his compensation, terms, conditions, or privileges of employment, because of such individual's race, color, religion, *sex*, or national origin.

At the time, most speculated that adding sex, or gender, to this list would act as a poison pill to kill the bill. The original legislation, drafted in 1963, was written to end racial discrimination. Representative Howard Smith, a Virginia segregationist, had previously gone on record as opposing any Civil Rights legislation. Yet, in his mischievous attempt to tank the bill, he introduced the one word amendment, "sex," into the bill in February 1964.

When he originally presented this to the House Floor for consideration, the Chamber broke out in laughter. The amusement was in part due to a letter Rep. Smith read aloud, which "presented statistics about the imbalance of men and women in the US population and called for the government to attend to the 'right' of unmarried women to find a husband."[9]

Separate from these unserious antics, there were many groups that supported the addition of "sex" to the bill, while others opposed it. The Civil Rights Bill passed the House by a 290–130 margin. In the Senate, Democrats staged a 75-day filibuster, and former KKK member Senator Robert Byrd droned on with a fourteen-hour filibuster to kill the bill. After a narrow margin vote to end the filibuster in the Senate, President Johnson signed the bill on July 2, 1964.[10]

This one-word amendment prank by Rep. Smith positively impacted the lives of more than half of the citizens of the United States, specifically women.

1979

1979 was another important year. That was the year I started my human resources professional career, turned 21 years old, and most importantly, when the US Pregnancy Discrimination Act went into effect.[11] Despite the Civil Rights Act of 1964, women were still being openly and legally discriminated against in the workplace. There was a gaping hole in the Civil Rights Act that did not protect women—women were being fired for getting pregnant and it was *legal*. In fact, women within their childbearing years were considered non-promotable. This meant that, prior to the Pregnancy Discrimination Act, women were legally denied promotional opportunities and intentionally left off succession plans for as long as 25 years despite their performance and capabilities!

When the Pregnancy Discrimination Act went into effect at last, the doors were wide open for women to be promoted based on their talent and performance. *Or so we thought.* When I entered leadership, it was a rather new frontier for women, and I faced some tough challenges. It didn't help that I worked at a shipyard, at a coal mine, and at petroleum pipelines, which were completely male-dominated at the time. Occasionally, I was blackballed or simply ignored by some of the male stakeholders I needed to deal with at those companies.

Back then, when it came to HR, women were always facing uphill battles—women like Edith, who was working for a pipeline competitor and interviewing for a position at our company. Edith was a candidate for a terminal manager position. She had a mechanical engineering degree and an MBA from the University of Tulsa. Plus, Edith had been working as a petroleum product terminal supervisor for a few years. She was a great fit for the job; however, she was slightly reserved during the interview. Edith did fine, but she did not oversell or come across boldly like many of the male candidates did.

We used panel interviews for employee selection in the 1980s, and I was the only female manager on the interview panel. During our discussion about Edith's qualifications for the position, a couple of the men said, "Well, she seems fairly capable, but she just doesn't have experience with us." *(What? Of course she didn't. She worked for another company—our competitor.)* The other panel members were more comfortable with the less-qualified male candidates. I fought hard, and in the end, Edith was hired. She accomplished much during her tenure, which outlasted mine. Edith rose to become the health, safety, and environmental director for a top energy company from which she recently retired.

When I was 31, I was promoted to corporate director of HR for the pipeline operation. I reported to the president of the business, which was an operating subsidiary of an energy company. Rest assured, the male internal candidates were not happy that I was selected for this position, as it was the most desirable HR operations position in the company. This was a peer role to refinery HR managers but had some better "perks" in the eyes of many. There was a lot of travel, as it covered 13 states of pipeline operations. There was also a corporate jet that I could reserve and use in this role as business needs dictated. My promotion as the only woman at this level in HR operations resulted in my being shunned by the HR corporate leadership team. For example, I received an invitation to the HR directors' offsite meeting—two weeks *after* the meeting was held.

Fortunately, my war stories are from decades ago, and I didn't allow those antics to stop me. The good news is that the workplace has improved in terms of *overt* negative treatment of women. Yet there is still much work to do.

So here we are today. I never imagined that, nearly *four decades* after the Pregnancy Discrimination Act passed, the number of CEO women at Fortune 500s would be under 7% and that women would only represent 11% of the highest earners at these corporations.[12]

What really stings is that *both* percentages have barely moved in the last two years since my book, *Fresh Insights to END the Glass Ceiling*, was released in August 2017.

Time for a Game-Changing Solution

The sad truth is that the majority of women are not even in the game, let alone on the same playing field as their male counterparts in regard to achieving the C-Suite positions. The stalled and declining numbers are proof of this.

The reason that the glass ceiling remains nearly impenetrable is that our assumptions and beliefs about the glass ceiling itself need to shift. Our misperceptions have resulted in designing solutions that are not delivering the necessary results. We are dabbling on the edges. It's time to make real progress and change.

It is hard to believe that 40 years have passed since the Pregnancy Discrimination Act, and the glass ceiling hasn't budged. Perhaps you're wondering why I care so much, since I am at the latter stages of my career and have succeeded as an entrepreneur and business owner. It is because my passion is leadership effectiveness and development. Frankly, there is still much to do. I remain energized about this work because I am confident we can rapidly make the necessary changes.

Also, this topic remains quite personal for me. I have two daughters with careers as high-level leaders, two daughters-in-law (one a surgeon and the other a dental hygienist), and three granddaughters. Patience is no longer virtuous for any of us when it comes to the glass ceiling. It needs to end because it is dysfunctional, continuing to hurt women as well as organizational performance.

This book will answer these elusive questions:

- Why is the glass ceiling firmly in place despite investments in women in leadership and diversity initiatives?

- What is really causing the glass ceiling?

- What are personality-based risks and how do they hurt leader performance and promotability?

- Why do women's risk as Worriers hold them back?

- Do men's risks as Egotists, Upstagers and Rule Breakers hurt them too?

- How can we deploy objective scientific methods to end the glass ceiling?

- Will promoting more women into senior leadership posts transform leadership and business performance?

- How can women manage their Worrier risk (and other risk factors) to develop their own talent more successfully? Do biased perceptions hurt women more than men?

- Which stakeholders can help? Is the C-Suite key?

- How can women have the power to end the glass ceiling?

THREE

Obstacles and Disconnects

"TACKLE the ROOT CAUSE not the EFFECT."
—*Haresh Sippy*

The Myths and the Blame Game

While the glass ceiling produces significant consequences for women and business profitability, the root causes have been elusive or misunderstood. As a result, advice frequently given to aspiring women leaders fails to help them break through barriers.

For example, Jack Welch, several years back, the former General Electric chairman and CEO, annoyed a group of female executives at a forum that was sponsored by the *Wall Street Journal*. He said that the only thing that could help women's advancement to senior executive positions is to "Over deliver . . . Performance is it!"[13] The female executives of the panel balked, accusing him of understanding nothing about cultural biases and how they shape the perception of performance.

Most would agree that Jack Welch has earned enough stripes as a leader to pontificate and speak anecdotally; however, we have empirical data that proves his response on this matter is misguided. Our data shows that women actually do dig in and work hard, and many push themselves even harder under pressure than their male counterparts. Sometimes women carry the brunt of the workload for their teams. Yet these same women are repeatedly overshadowed and bypassed for the best and most coveted positions.

Additionally, a 2015 Pew Research Center study of 1,835 adult respondents stated: "About four-in-ten Americans point to a double standard for women seeking to climb to the highest levels of either politics or business, where they have to do more than their male counterparts to prove themselves."

Lack of Traction with Diversity Initiatives

Clearly, companies are investing heavily in diversity and inclusion endeavors, to the tune of $8 billion a year spent on diversity training alone.[14] Keep in mind, the hottest jobs on the market are "diversity and inclusion" executives with a salary range between $146,698 and $223,163 (2018).[15] Unfortunately, at this point the results are falling short. Boston Consulting Group's 2017 study of 17,500 employees found that 91% of women interviewed said they were aware of the gender-diversity initiatives offered at their company, yet only 27% said they have benefitted from them.[16]

According to the *Harvard Business Review* article, "Why Diversity Programs Fail," Frank Dobbin and Alexandra Kelav state:

> It shouldn't be surprising that most diversity programs aren't increasing diversity. Despite a few new bells and whistles, courtesy of big data, companies are basically doubling down on the same approaches they've used since the 1960s—which often make things worse, not better. . . . One major reason is that three-quarters use negative messages in their training. By headlining the legal case for diversity and trotting out stories of huge settlements, they issue an implied threat: 'Discriminate, and the company will pay the price.' We understand the temptation—that's how we got your attention in the first paragraph—but threats, or 'negative incentives,' don't win converts.[17]

In terms of diversity training, as reported in an article in the *World Economic Forum:*

> The US government is training every one of its 2.8 million employees to avoid unconscious bias. Starbucks is planning to close more than eight thousand stores for the day to give its staff similar courses. In the UK, the government has already trained a hundred thousand civil servants and recommends that every major employer do the same.[18]

More and more companies are investing in similar ways. According to Odette Chalaby author of "Diversity Training Doesn't Change People's Behaviour. We Need to Find Out What Does," the only problem is that these efforts won't work:

> Unconscious bias training is often given to managers in charge of hiring and promotion. It's meant to reveal to them their hidden prejudices and biases, usually towards women or ethnic minorities, and educate them about the impact that bias has on decision-making.
>
> But study after study has shown that while training may raise awareness of prejudice, it doesn't change people's behaviour at all.[19]

Odette Chalaby concludes:

> But don't offer diversity training, unconscious bias training, or leadership training for female employees, because there's no evidence that they work. Don't bother with diverse selection panels. Sometimes they may help female candidates, but sometimes they harm them.[20]

The point is: today's methods are not producing the results we need. I don't agree that we should abandon the diversity and women-in-leadership initiatives, we just have to design and deliver them differently. We must also begin by educating senior leaders about the reality of the glass ceiling and how high the financial stakes are. Once these top executives truly grasp how ending the glass ceiling is a profoundly profitable business opportunity, they *will* champion the change.

Cultural Quake: #MeToo, the Kavanaugh Case, and the Gender Diversity Imperative

The push of gender diversity to increase the number of women in top executive positions has been long past due. If we wish to succeed, however, it matters how we push.

As stated earlier, an unintended consequence of the #MeToo movement and Judge Kavanaugh hearings is the trampling of progress for women in leadership. Men are becoming increasingly more fearful of sexual harassment, discrimination lawsuits, and even being accused of microaggressions.

In the *Women in the Workplace 2018* comprehensive study by McKinsey,[21] authors point out that "women face everyday discrimination and ongoing microaggressions." Some of the microaggressions they cited as "perceived" sexism seemed flawed. One example of a microaggression from the study was "a man mistakenly assumed a woman coworker was more junior than she really was." In another perceived case of a microaggression from the study, a female Latina executive shared,

> One thing I've become used to is having to prove myself constantly, over and over. It's tiring, and unfortunately it hasn't changed a whole lot as I've become more senior.

In both cases, there may be other reasons for these concerns that negate them from being acts of microaggressions. In the first example, assuming someone is more junior can happen for a myriad of reasons. Perhaps the relationship is new or distant. Perhaps the woman has a youthful appearance. Perhaps the man saying this does not have adequate background information about the woman. Perhaps the woman stays in the background, rarely speaks up, and lacks visibility.

The mind-set of the Latina female executive who believes she must constantly prove herself correlates with our research about women. It may suggest that her need to repeatedly prove herself comes from her own inner doubts and self-perception rather than anyone else's external perceptions, expectations, or demands. This is not to disregard the fact that acts of "real" discrimination occur daily in organizations and need to be addressed in timely, fair, and decisive ways.

However, we add fuel to the fire of gender inequity in leadership if we proceed with overlabeling or accusing every slight or perceived infraction as discrimination or as a microaggression. This creates finger-pointing, blaming, and a defensive environment and mind-set for all. It forms and fosters a victim mentality for women. Men walk on eggshells around women rather than building effective and supportive relationships. It becomes difficult to work together as open communications shut down. Ultimately, it is negative, unproductive, and unhelpful. If we default to these automatic assumptions of discrimination, we hurt the development, growth, and success of the very people we want to support.

Unfortunately, mistrust is growing. It is essential that we counteract it by fostering supportive environments where everyone is thriving and included so that we may rebuild trusting relationships. The solutions to the glass ceiling cultivate trust and maximize business performance. A big part of building and maintaining trusting relationships relies on the following elements:

- Acting with Fairness and Objectivity
- Always Showing Respect
- Demonstrating Openness / Transparency
- Offering Support
- Showing Concern / Empathy
- Showing Trust in Others
- Using Active Listening
- Valuing Others

Google's Firing of James Damore:
Is the Pendulum Swinging Too Far?

"If we cannot have an honest discussion about this,
then we can never truly solve the problem."

—*James Damore*

In late 2017, Google fired James Damore. This was troubling on a couple of levels. He was fired for writing and submitting a 3,300-word manifesto complaining about preferential treatment toward women. Here are excerpts from Damore's introduction:

> I value diversity and inclusion, am not denying that sexism exists, and don't endorse using stereotypes. When addressing the gap in representation in the population, we need to look at population level differences in distributions. If we can't have an honest discussion about this, then we can never truly solve the problem. . . . People generally have good intentions, but we all have biases which are invisible to us. Thankfully, open and honest discussion with those who disagree can highlight our blind spots and help us grow, which is why I wrote this document. Google has several biases and honest discussion about these biases is being silenced by the dominant ideology. What follows is by no means the complete story, but it's a perspective that desperately needs to be told at Google.[22]

As mentioned earlier, during the first half of my career, I was an HR leader at line operations. Having an open-door policy at the operating companies where I served was perhaps the most important communication tool we had. This Open Door Policy was a critical lifeline of communication for employees to report any problems when I worked in employee relations at a union-free coal mine in Gillette, Wyoming. In fact, the company was so serious about this that we called it the "Direct Line," since all messages went directly to the mine manager, who was the top official at the coal mine. In this way, no one could interfere with a message, not even employee relations.

From an HR perspective, I cannot imagine firing an employee who complained or gave his or her opinion in a respectful way—even if it was a bit off base—by expressing a disagreement with company policy. I can assure you that I have received some bizarre feedback and letters in my time in HR, and I still cannot fathom what Google did in response to Damore.

NANCY E. PARSONS

For example, one mechanic was angry that we hired an unmarried female mechanic—he felt men should have been hired instead because they had families to feed. *What?* We did not fire or discipline him. Rather, we worked on educating our employees and managers on our policies and the *whys* behind them. We also held employees accountable for treating each other with respect. This is perhaps the most important policy a company can implement. I personally worked with employees to help them understand that all junior employees needed mentoring and support—no matter their race, gender, ethnicity, or background. Of course, in the mining industry, employees' lives could depend on counting on one another in an emergency situation.

With Google, both the company and the employee were correct in some areas but lacking in others. Google, it appears (and I am writing this from media reports, reading Damore's Manifesto, and without any access to the company's personnel records), has good intentions of promoting women, and they are quite serious and diligent in how they implement and enforce their diversity initiatives. One can also assume James Damore, the software engineer who was fired, had good intentions by trying to let the company know his perception regarding the impact of their policies by writing an obviously thoughtful piece.

After circulating his manifesto, Damore was fired by Google. CEO Sundar Pichai, who cut short his vacation due to the media fallout, denounced Damore's memo for "advancing harmful stereotypes." *Really?*

Whether we agree or disagree with Damore's comments, it turns out that some of his points about observable gender differences or reactions when the pressure is high, are correct, according to our research.

Let me clarify before I jump off the cliff of the politically incorrect abyss. I am, and always have been, dedicated to ending not only the glass ceiling, but also discrimination, harassment, and negative bias that hurts women, minorities, and other groups of individuals.

Like it or not, our scientific personality research generally agrees with a key part of Mr. Damore's contention: women under stress and conflict are more neurotic, so to speak, and tend to be Worriers more often than men.

Experiencing or perceiving women as more neurotic than men when facing tough challenges is not a sexist stereotype or a figment of Mr. Damore's imagination. This Worrier trait is real, and it holds many women back when the heat is on. Although he claims it is biological—a point I would argue—the personality data on this behavior is clear.

Expanding the Dialogue

The point is, discussing this topic and expressing opposing views, in my mind, is healthy and necessary. Men and women need to feel comfortable exploring the issues, concerns, differences, and scientific data. They should not have to fear being let go for not staying in line with a company policy that may have stretched too far with the intent to be fair or to correct past inequities.

In our quest to rapidly prepare and promote more women, the last thing we need to be doing is unduly opposing men or acting as the gender thought police. We should not assume that gender bias is the predominate reason why women are not reaching top positions. We should not put effort into developing only women and minorities. If we forge forward with win-win solutions, this will allow us to make the necessary inroads. The goal is to lift the barriers for women and promote all candidates based on well-constructed leadership competencies and expectations. This should not be done while excluding or penalizing men who are well suited and qualified. We need inclusivity for all. Today's competency models are flawed and can be modified to naturally welcome and support diverse talent. If we remove the barriers to entry and promotion, diversely rich and talented people—both men and women—will succeed.

Men's Views on the Glass Ceiling

We can't ignore the perceptions of men—in particular, those of most male executives who, because it's not personal for them, don't recognize the glass ceiling or see the true magnitude of how it impacts the bottom line. Most male executives go through the motions of sponsoring and supporting "diversity councils" and "women-in-leadership initiatives" at a distance, but these actions are not producing the change and the sustainable impact needed to end the glass ceiling. "Diversity" and "women in leadership" are convenient functional responsibilities to pass on to others. In this way, male C-Suite members are able to check the box that they are doing something about ending the glass ceiling, allowing them to focus on "more important" or "real" business issues.

In the 2016 PayScale survey with about 140,000 people from a broad range of industries, it was reported that 67% of men believe that in most workplaces "men and women have equal opportunities." Yet only 38% of women say that's the case.[23] Clearly, men have a more difficult time seeing the magnitude of the problem.

What do men in business think in general? Results of another survey conducted of over 300 full-time working men in the US, a mix of managers and professionals in mid-to-late career and in a variety of industries including hi-tech and finance, are telling. When asked about women being treated unfairly in the workplace, most responded: "It's a problem, just *not* where I work."

> While a full one-third of men think women are treated unfairly in the workplace in general, just 10% of respondents agree that women are treated unfairly in *their* workplace. In other words, the men we spoke to don't believe that gender bias happens in their own backyard."[24]

When you add to men's lack of serious focus on this topic, the #MeToo movement, and Kavanaugh hearings, male leaders are now less inclined to mentor or facilitate the growth of high-potential women due to fear of reprisals or potential accusations of misbehavior. Yet, it is imperative that men executives support—and champion—ending the glass ceiling. The Boston Consulting Group (2018) reports "that among companies where men are actively involved in gender diversity initiatives, *96% report progress.* Conversely, among companies where men are not involved, only 30% show progress."[25] We can create win-win solutions.

Whenever I present at leadership conferences on the topic, "Fresh Insights to End the Glass Ceiling," men leaders seldom attend. Women fill the rooms. This demonstrates that the glass ceiling is simply not a topic of keen interest or a serious matter for most men. They usually only attend when they are required to for mandated diversity and sexual harassment training.

Apathy about the glass ceiling isn't a mind-set for only the mature men well into their leadership careers. According to a Harvard University poll of young Americans reported in 2016:

> When 18- to 29-year-olds were asked whether a glass ceiling (a barrier to advancement in a profession) exists for women in America today, nearly three in five (59%) indicated yes. Young women are significantly more likely to believe a glass ceiling exists (68%), compared to men (50%).[26]

Young men are less inclined than young women to believe that women still face the glass ceiling. It's not personal for them, and therefore, they don't tend to notice. A cynical view would be that as we correct this obstacle for women, men in turn would achieve fewer coveted positions. An optimistic view would say that there is plenty of opportunity for all who achieve and perform well as leaders because business opportunities will expand. I prefer the latter point of view, or the "blue ocean" way of thinking.

Tokenism Is NOT the Answer

"Tokenism . . . the policy or practice of making only a symbolic effort . . . (such as hiring a person who belongs to a minority group) only to prevent criticism and give the appearance that people are being treated fairly.

—*Merriam-Webster*

Tokenism is still very much in play. Too often, we see women promoted to executive positions who do not meet the qualifications or who are not well-suited for the executive post. Male executives sometimes select what we refer to as "pleasers"—obedient or reserved female administrators who will execute and follow orders as needed without causing any trouble. Furthermore, they fulfill the diversity requirement, another box men executives can check off. While this does not represent the majority of women in executive positions today, there are still too many who are promoted due to their gender and agreeableness versus their talent, capability, creativity, boldness, and true leadership forte. Tokenism hinders progress for women and fosters the self-fulfilling prophecy about the lackluster capability of women in leadership.

Frequently, the C-Suite's "token" women are hired into chief human resource positions. This actually sends two bad business messages: 1) the senior leadership team lacks sincerity about promoting highly capable, talented women, and 2) human resources is not a serious priority. In the cases where a token is hired, there are typically agreeable women who will not rock the boat, champion change and progress, or challenge the status quo.

Here are three cases that may sound familiar: I know of a CHRO who came from an accounting/finance background and then into HR and was, unsurprisingly, an extreme introvert. For years, she stayed in the background for this large transportation firm and acted from behind the scenes. She remained quiet on key issues at leadership meetings. She eventually developed a dysfunctional brigade of passive-aggressive female directors who reported to her and wreaked havoc in the organization. The CHRO stayed in the distance, ignoring the dysfunction in her organization and the repeated turnover of the best talent. She stayed in this role for many years, and the department's reputation and performance suffered the entire time.

Another CHRO, this one in the energy industry at a Fortune 100 company, was a micromanager and an extreme perfectionist. She could not let anyone in her department make a decision without her involvement. She was also oddly frugal, in one instance refusing to allow trainers to hire a bellman to help with many boxes in order to avoid the extra expense of paying the tip. She was eventually let go and the department and stakeholders all breathed a sigh of relief.

A third CHRO, unlike the two I mentioned above, was a victim and complainer. She saw the differences between herself and her male C-Suite team members as detrimental. She had a terrible chip on her shoulder, focusing on her own perceived lack of power instead of building her department's vision and success, and constantly complained or made snide remarks in the presence of the senior team. She was never a strong fit for the position, and rather than put her best foot forward, she would wallow in resentment, suspicion, and self-pity. She was soon forced out of the role.

In all three cases, these women were selected for the wrong reasons. They were selected mostly for their gender and not because they were top candidates or great fits for their respective jobs. Tokenism is not only detrimental to women and minorities but to the business and every stakeholder. It is a misguided solution to meeting diversity goals and is taking us the wrong direction to end the glass ceiling. Therefore, tokenism should be abolished immediately.

Sexual Harassment, Bullying, and Likely Victims

*"You're not a victim for sharing your story. You are
a survivor setting the world on fire with your truth.
And you never know who needs your light, your
warmth, and raging courage."*

—Alex Elle

Sexual harassment is another factor hindering our movement towards ending the glass ceiling. Thankfully, the #MeToo movement has exposed the gravity and pervasiveness of the problem. The media, entertainment industry, and US political systems fester with cases of sexual harassment and abuse from decades ago through to the present day. No sector is free of these unlawful predatory behaviors. While the focus of this book is not sexual harassment, there are some parallels to leadership effectiveness and the glass ceiling phenomena.

I've interviewed scores of executive women throughout the past couple of years and asked them if they have ever been sexually harassed on the job. All but one have replied with a resounding *no*. This defies the studies we see on the incident rate of sexual harassment. Pew Research reports from a 2018 survey that

> 59% of women and 27% of men say that they have personally received unwanted sexual advances or verbal or physical harassment of a sexual nature whether in or outside of a work context. . . . Overall, 69% of the women (of the 59%) who say they have experienced sexual harassment say this happened in a work setting.[27]

If we were to add bullying to the discussion, the numbers are worse.

> Almost 75% of employees surveyed had been affected by workplace bullying. The 2017 US Workplace Bullying Survey showed that almost 60% of US workers are affected by it. . . . workplace bullying is not equally split between men (70%) and women (30%), women tend to bully more women than men (more than 65% in both cases). Studies have also shown that women can carry unconscious bias against women.[28]

Sexual harassment and bullying behaviors come from a similar place. Excessive aggressiveness, lack of compassion and empathy, self-indulgence, narcissism, impulsive risk-taking, and mean-spiritedness are some of the common characteristics of these perpetrators. While a lack of compassion and empathy are measured in our CDR Character Assessment, many of the darker aspects are identifiable within our CDR Risk Assessment.

In our research presented in this book, we focus on the inherent risk factors. That is where the key differences between men and women, ones that impact the glass ceiling, are found. The men leaders generally tended to have a "*Moving Against*" or aggressive profile under stress and adversity. Meanwhile, the women tended to "*Move Away*." Keep in mind that while these aggressive behaviors by men are the norm, only a very small percentage of men leaders are harassers or bullies. Women leaders who have "moving against" trends can also be abusive, albeit in extremely low numbers.

Interestingly, the female executives I interviewed who had never been sexually harassed have *Moving Against* profiles. They lack the "victim" profile. They are fighters who stand their ground.

Our firm is conducting a research study on sexual harassment and bullying based on one's inherent risk factors. It is clear that women who are Worriers and Pleasers—*Moving Away* without fighting back from adversity or conflict—are more likely to be victims of sexual harassment and bullying. If we are able to confirm the personality-based differences of potential victims, we can identify those with these traits early on. With this research and identification, we can equip these more likely victims with the necessary education and training early on so they may develop skills and tactics to remain strong amidst unacceptable or unlawful advances and behaviors. We can also identify potential aggressors and be sure to hold them accountable. Let's bring an end to ignoring and protecting these toxic behaviors by using objective scientific measures.

Lack of Leadership Accountability

As mentioned in the Introduction, with the staggering ineffective rates of leaders ranging from 50% – 75%, there is much work to do. A large part of these ineffective rates are due to inherent risk factor behaviors running amok in organizations. This means that the 11 unproductive coping behaviors CDR has identified undermine leadership success. This can and must change.

When it comes to leadership effectiveness, the single most important thing a leader can do is show that they respect each person who works for them and all stakeholders. Leaders need to show their employees that they are valued. Expressing gratitude that each employee chose to work for the company and appreciating their contributions is a start; however, showing respect and striving to build trusting relationships is essential to be an effective leader. Today, in most organizations, leaders are not held accountable for demonstrating respect toward others. Turning the other cheek, pretending all is well, looking only at financial performance, and supporting dysfunctional risk behaviors needs to end.

A witch hunt is not the way to go; we simply need decency and accountability to prevail. If executives balk at these two basic requirements, are they fit to lead?

Psychological Safety, Tolerance, and Respect

"Psychological safety is a belief that one will not be punished or humiliated for speaking up with ideas, questions, concerns or mistakes."
—Amy Edmondson

Clearly, *all employees need to be respected and valued*, welcomed to express different opinions and ideas. While some may miss the mark, shutting down discussions, thoughts, and opposing views is detrimental, fostering resentment and mistrust. In the case of James Damore at Google, the notion that he was fired for "supporting dangerous stereotypes" is absurd. Again, his research and conclusions may have not been completely accurate, but he appeared to have good intentions and had given thought and care to his argument.

Psychological safety applies to women and men alike. If everyone is fearful, walking on eggshells, or overly sensitive about every minor comment, perceived slight, or action, building trust and respect cannot happen. If women wear their emotions on their sleeves and executive men continue to avoid mentoring or spending time with their female employees, this hurts women and performance. Learning to tolerate and welcome the differences in opinion helps to create a truly diverse work environment. This works well when trust and respect are the foundation.

FOUR

Performance: Do the Math!

"Great leaders are not defined by the absence of weakness,
but rather by the presence of clear strengths."

—John Zenger

We don't even need to talk about the glass ceiling or the gender inequities in leadership. We can go straight to performance and the bottom line. These are the concepts most important to today's executives and, more importantly, shareholders. While businesses exist for a multitude of purposes, achieving monetary goals is a must for them to continue to exist and prosper.

Can Women Lead as Effectively as Men?

The short answer is—absolutely! Studies compiled by the American Psychological Association repeatedly show that "one's sex has little or no bearing on personality, cognition, and leadership." [29] Our CDR Character Assessment data supports this finding.

Performance Results of Women in Leadership

Study after study shows that the more women hold senior leadership positions, the better the company's performance.

In the case of 360° leader performance feedback,

> When reviewing performance, many may find this data astonishing: Women leaders are frequently rated higher on multirater 360° feedback than their male counterparts. In fact, Jack Zenger and Joseph Folkman reported in their 2011 survey of 7,280 leaders that 'at all levels, women are *rated higher in fully 12 of the 16 competencies* that go into outstanding leadership.' [30]

Considering cases of return on equity,

> A study of 4,000 public companies from across the globe, published by MSCI Research in 2015, found that 'companies that had strong female leadership generated a Return on Equity of 10.1% per year versus 7.4% for those without.' [31]

In another persuasive case,

> In a study of its $23 billion global lending portfolio, Calvert determined that companies with the most women in senior

leadership positions—the people who report directly to the CEO—delivered *double the average annual return* on equity over the last 11 years compared with the companies with the fewest.

Calvert saw better performance when women comprised anywhere between 33% – 75% of the leadership, she said. Firms with the fewest women in senior management—20% or less—returned on average 4.4% per year. Those with the most—more than 57% women—returned 8.6%. [32]

And then,

Take this provocative recent analysis from Boston-based trading firm Quantopian. Between 2002 and 2014, researchers compared the returns of Fortune 1000 companies led by female CEOs to those of the S&P 500. During that time period, the companies with women at the helm saw retu*rns that were 226% higher.* [33]

Reported in a *Forbes* article that cited a study from UC Davis,

Among the 25 firms with the highest percentage of women execs and board members, researchers found that median returns on assets and equity in 2015 were at least 74% higher than among the overall group of companies surveyed. [34]

The largest global study confirms when there are more women at senior levels, companies perform better. As noted in the Introduction of this book,

The hard-hitting report released in 2016 by Peterson Institute for International Economics was based on a peer review study of 21,980 companies from 91 countries where it was reported that Companies with at least 30% female leaders—in senior management positions—experienced a 15% increase in profitability. (Note: these results are based on a typical company with an average 6.4% net margin.) [35]

Case made.

LEADEROCRITY®

I coined the term "LEADEROCRITY®" as a palatable way of say-ing leadership needs to vastly improve. This is the focus of my book, *Transforming LEADEROCRITY*®, slated for 2020 publication. I've used descriptions for my presentations like "Leadership is Broken" and have had association conferences change my title because it was too negative. I continue to be told by marketing specialists (and find in the real world too) that "negative," doesn't sell, even if it is the truth.

When Kim and I founded CDR in 1998, leadership was funda-mentally broken, with studies back then showing 50% – 75% of lead-ers as ineffective. This trend continues. Here are the findings of four recent studies.

1. According to a 2017 Society of Human Resource Manage-ment report: "Statistics show that in the first 18 months of taking a leadership position, 30% – 70% of leaders fail. These failures cost companies a lot—in time, valuable resources and money. Research shows that costs to replace senior ex-ecutives can range from $750,000 to $2.5 million, and up to $52 million for a CEO. In addition, turnover at the top can generate indirect costs such as increased employee stress and decreased employee engagement." [36]

2. The Center for Creative Leadership reports research that shows 50% of leaders and managers are "estimated to be ineffective, incompetent or a mis-hire." [37]

3. A survey by 14,000 HR professionals found that only 26% thought the quality of leadership in their company was ex-cellent or very good. [38]

4. "Companies fail to choose the candidate with the right talent for the job 82% of the time," according to the Gallup article "Why Great Managers Are So Rare." If great managers seem scarce, it's because the talent required to be one is rare. Gal-lup's research reveals that about one in 10 people possess the talent to manage. Though many people are endowed with some of the necessary traits, few have the unique combina-tion of talent needed to help a team achieve excellence in a way that significantly improves a company's performance.

This 10%, when put in manager roles, naturally engages team members and customers, retains top performers, and sustains a culture of high productivity.[39]

The Math

This is not rocket science, although it is an elusive business blind spot and organizational struggle. Let's do some basic math from a macro perspective. In 2017, the US netted corporate profits of $2.1 trillion.[40] Again, studies have consistently shown that between 50% – 75% of leaders are ineffective. If we were to improve effectiveness and related profits by 30%, that would be $630 billion. The amount of potential profit lost by today's organizations is mind-boggling. However, what a tremendous opportunity! What is so ironic is that we have the necessary talent hiding in front of us (women) in all organizations.

Time for Change

Clearly, the first key step to seizing this opportunity and improving leadership performance is to *promote more women*. The research and solutions in this book will prepare women and organizations to take this course to improve performance and, as a result, financial success.

FIVE

About the Research

"Research is creating new knowledge."
—Neil Armstrong

About CDR Assessment Group, Inc. and the Assessments Used in the Study

When we formed CDR in 1998, our vision was to revolutionize leadership. After our unexpected research findings, helping women to break through the glass ceiling clearly became part of our vision as well.

My business partner, Kimberly Leveridge, PhD, and I developed the CDR Character Assessment and CDR Risk Assessment in 1998, and early the next year released the CDR Drivers & Rewards Assessment, completing the CDR 3-Dimensional Assessment Suite®. To this day, due to the level of detail and nuanced characteristics revealed, these assessments are considered by many to be unmatched coaching tools. They have been used in every business sector by thousands of leaders around the globe.

The CDR 3-D Suite is primarily used for executive coaching and for leadership and team development. However, many of our clients also use these tools for selection and succession planning since the tools are scientifically validated for these purposes as well.

For the research in this book, we focused primarily on the study results using the CDR Risk Assessment, which identifies personality-based risks that can lead to derailment. Secondly, we used the CDR Character Assessment, which measures the inherent strengths, or positive personality traits, of the respective groups.

Personality assessment is useful for describing an individual's characteristics that might not be directly observed. Behaviors are visible to people, but the reasons behind them and the motivations for them are not observable. Psychological assessment results provide a vocabulary for describing propensities and a view of the *whys* behind the behaviors. This information in turn allows for more effective employee selection, succession planning, team building, and professional development.

CDR Character Assessment

This personality instrument identifies individual distinctions and measures leader acumen, vocational suitability or "best fit" roles, emotional intelligence, key strengths, and potential gaps or short sides. This assessment describes the compelling and impactful performance and behavior implications of an individual's character attributes from a business and leadership development perspective.

Table 1 shows the CDR Character Assessment scales and what each character trait measures.

TABLE 1

CDR Character Assessment Scale Titles and Descriptions

CHARACTER SCALE* TITLE	DESCRIPTION OF THE CHARACTER TRAIT
Adjustment	Calm, self-assured, and steady under pressure versus self-critical, edgy, and an intense performer
Leadership Energy	Inclined to take charge, be leader-like, interested in upward career mobility, and highly competitive versus having tendencies to avoid leadership roles, directing others, and interacting with those that are not concerned with upward mobility as a measure for success
Sociability	Is outgoing, extroverted, enjoys social interaction, stimulated by dialoging with others versus having more introverted tendencies such as preferring less social interaction, maintaining a lower profile, keeping to oneself, and being quiet and perhaps shy
Interpersonal Sensitivity	Warm, caring, sensitive toward the needs of others, interpersonally skilled and perceptive versus task focused, hard-nosed, and apathetic toward the needs of others
Prudence	Practical, conscientious, self-controlled and disciplined, steady, reliable, stable, and logical in a steadfast way versus spontaneous, risk-taking, adventurous, potentially creative, adaptable, and inventive
Inquisitive	Adventurous, clever, original, creative, imaginative, and curious versus practical, task and process focused, detail oriented, and more down-to-earth
Learning Approach	Typically seeks learning for the sake of personal enrichment and has academic interests versus being more interested in practical educational approaches such as on-the-job training and hands-on learning

SOURCE: Nancy Parsons and Kimberly Leveridge, PhD, *CDR Character Assessment* (CDR Assessment Group, Inc., 1998).

*Regarding the above character assessment scales, each of these scales has many subscales in the actual report that provide for more robust individual differentiation during the coaching and development process.

CDR Risk Assessment

This personality measure identifies 11 inherent risk factors and related behaviors that can erode performance and lead to derailment. Gone unchecked, these risks can drive even the most promising careers off track. It is important to recognize one's own risks in order to develop, neutralize, or manage them more productively.

Table 2 shows the CDR Risk Assessment Factors and what each risk factor measures.

TABLE 2
CDR Assessment Risk Factors

RISK FACTOR SCALE TITLE	DESCRIPTION OF THE RISK FACTOR
False Advocate	Has passive-aggressive tendencies, appears outwardly supportive while covertly resisting
Worrier	Demonstrates unwillingness to make decisions due to fear of failure or criticism
Cynic	Is skeptical, mistrustful, pessimistic, always looking for problems, constantly questions decisions, resists innovation
Rule Breaker	Ignores rules, tests the limits, does what feels good, risks company resources, does not think through consequences
Perfectionist	Micromanages, clings to details, has a high need to control, has compulsive tendencies, sets unreasonably high standards
Egotist	Is self-centered, has a sense of entitlement and superiority, takes credit for others' accomplishments, is a hard-nosed competitor

Table 2 continues on the next page.

TABLE 2 (CONTINUED)
CDR Assessment Risk Factors

RISK FACTOR SCALE TITLE	DESCRIPTION OF THE RISK FACTOR
Pleaser	Depends on others for feedback and approval, is eager to please the boss, avoids making decisions alone, won't challenge status quo, refuses to rock the boat
Hyper-Moody	Has unpredictable emotional swings, moodiness, volatility, potentially explosive outbursts, and vacillation of focus
Detached	Withdraws, fades away, fails to communicate, avoids confrontation, is aloof, tunes others out
Upstager	Is excessively dramatic and histrionic, dominates meetings and airtime, constantly sells a personal vision and viewpoint, demonstrates inability to go with the tide
Eccentric	Quite unusual in their thinking and behavior, perhaps whimsical, weird, out of social step or norms, peculiar in some ways

SOURCE: Nancy Parsons and Kimberly Leveridge, PhD CDR Assessment Group, Inc., 1998.

Our Original Study Was Not About the Glass Ceiling

We were originally conducting research comparing 360° Leader Scan™ multi-rater performance feedback results to the CDR Character and Risk Assessment data.[41] Unexpectedly, we found stark, statistically significant differences in the CDR Risk Assessment results between men and women leaders. This propelled us to begin to look more closely at the gender-based differences and launch our research into the glass ceiling.

Research Overview

1. In part one of our research, we compared inherent personality risk assessment results from the CDR Risk Assessment of men and women leader study groups.

2. Next, we compared CDR Character and Risk Assessment results with Pew Cultural Survey results regarding the gender perceptions.

3. We then analyzed the CDR study groups' personality data (character and risks) with corporate executive women and CEO women groups.

4. Lastly, in late 2018, we analyzed the Western European (IE. edu) study of women leaders and men leaders.

The Study Participants

In the first part of the study, we reviewed the CDR Risk Assessment results of mid-level leaders: 137 women and 122 men from thirty-five companies from North America (the results are discussed in Chapter 6 and fully presented in Chapter 16). In 2018, we completed the analysis of the Western European men and women leaders with 145 women leaders and 294 men leaders.

In the second part of our study, we analyzed the personality assessment results of 30 corporate executive women and 21 female CEO/entrepreneurs who were members in Executive Women's Forum

(EWF) International groups (results are also discussed in Chapter 6 and fully presented in Chapter 16). Leaders in each of our studies were from more than eighty companies. The executive women's group from Western Europe was not a large enough sample size with only 6 women in this group.

2018 Research: IE Business School (IE.edu) Study of Western Europe Executives and Leaders

Marta Williams, who is a globally recognized master executive coach and professor—along with Stephen Adamson, currently a director within the Executive Education Department at IE Business School located in Madrid, Spain—presented the results of a two-year study at the "Hay Festival for Leadership in the 21st Century." They shared the leadership behaviors of nearly 500 leaders and executives from throughout Western Europe. The measures they used to look at this were the CDR 3-D Suite including the CDR Character Assessment, CDR Risk Assessment, and the CDR Drivers & Rewards Assessment. My team at CDR supported them with this research.

Their purpose was to look at today's leaders (primarily in Western Europe) and executives to identify styles and needs for the future. They asked: What behavioral weaknesses are most likely to derail their careers? And, how can we help them to reach their maximum potential? They also sought to explore whether there were notable differences between the leadership strengths of men and women executives.

Their inquiry was of great interest to my team to see if the Western European results were similar to the primarily North America based data used in my book *Fresh Insights to END the Glass Ceiling*.

For some background, Marta Williams and Stephen Adamson have created a unique personal development program for more than 600 executives and leaders studying at Madrid's IE Business School. Since 2016, these executives and leader participants have received a creative combination coaching feedback with specialized psychometric testing, in-depth analysis of their leadership styles, and feedback from their coworkers. Measurements were conducted on a continuous basis to track growth and perceptions of change from multiple points of view.

The gender-based findings for the CDR Risk Assessment for the IE leaders and executives include 145 women leaders (out of a total of

445 executives and leadership participants) and six executive women. While the sample size of the executive women is small (N=6), we view it as a trend and compare it to trends of executive/CEO women in our original North American studies.

Pew Cultural Survey: Women and Leadership

The Pew Cultural Survey Report of 2015 referenced in this book is a summary of key trends throughout the movement of women into leadership positions in politics, business, and other labor force professions. In Chapter 13, I will introduce the cultural bias of men versus women and then compare these Pew Survey results to CDR Personality Assessment results. The Pew Survey obtained results from telephone interviews with a nationally representative sample of 2,250 adults living in the continental United States.

2018 Pew Research: How Men and Women View Gender in Leadership

The 2018 Pew Social Trends[42] study, a newer study specifically about perceptions of women and men leaders, shows how perceptions of the capability of men and women leaders is viewed in the US. Data in this report are drawn from the panel wave conducted within June 19 – July 2, 2018, among 4,587 respondents. The margin of sampling error for the full group of 4,587 respondents is plus or minus 2.4 percentage points.

More details about the personality research results can be found in Chapter 16. The Pew Survey results are described in Chapter 13. Information about research methodology, assessments, and validity, as well as the Pew Surveys, can be found in Appendix I.

SIX

The Root Cause

"Worrying is an inkblot over life's wonderful itinerary."
—Erwin D. Maramat

CDR has spent two decades measuring the personality and motivational traits of leaders and executives. Interestingly, the overall leadership characteristics or inherent personality strengths—as measured by our CDR Character Assessment—between men and women leaders are remarkably similar. This means that both sexes are quite capable of the highest leadership positions. This supports the previously mentioned APA studies set forth in their publication, "Men and Women: No Big Difference." [43]

The "Break-Through" Finding

As mentioned in Chapter 1, our "break-through" (pun intended) to ending the glass ceiling came as a result of research conducted using the CDR Risk Assessment, which revealed that a preponderance of women are "Worriers." Secondarily, perceptions and biases also help fortify the glass ceiling. In Chapter 13, we will explore why the bias issue is far more damaging and pervasive than most think. First, however, I will reveal our exciting research findings that provide a much clearer path to implementable solutions.

A Summary of the Glass Ceiling Research Findings

#1 — Women Leaders Are "Worriers"

Most illuminating and new in our research findings is that most women leaders are "Worriers," and that this self-defeating risk factor is holding the glass ceiling firmly in place. This means that

> **women pull *themselves* out of the running for promotions and upward mobility.**

Research shows that women tend to *Move Away* from conflict and adversity. By failing to stand their ground, they lose visibility and hurt their credibility. Ironically, when facing adversity and pressure, women do what Jack Welch suggested—they dig in, work harder, outperform, analyze, research, often become sleep deprived, and work harder again. Many women tend to spend too much time overanalyzing and studying versus engaging in the tough leadership discussions necessary for advancement. Women often fear speaking up when they most need to do so. (These results were from our initial study of 137 mid-level leaders across 35 companies in North America.)

#2 — Men Leaders Are "Egotists," "Rule Breakers," and "Upstagers"

While many women leaders scored high as Worriers, their male counterparts in the North America-based study showed a statistically significant difference in their CDR Risk Assessment results. Male leaders tended to be Egotists, Rule Breakers, and Upstagers under adversity and conflict. These risk factors result in their using aggression, forcefulness, and assertive or *Moving Against* behaviors. This makes them seem courageous and therefore seemingly more promotable or leader-like.

Men win the perception battle by having the stamina to stay in the game and fight to the end. During conflict or adverse situations, male leaders will do what it takes to succeed, even if it defies the rules of appropriate behavioral standards for leaders. Even though certain behaviors are dysfunctional or divisive, they are typically either viewed favorably or ignored when exhibited by men.

#3 — Women CEOs and Corporate Executives' Risks Are More Like Men's Risks

The big takeaway here is that the women who are making it to the top levels in organizations exhibit risks similar to the men's leader group. So, when a woman's risk behaviors are the types men have, she has a chance to make it to the top. If not, her career will likely be stalled or stopped prematurely.

Women CEOs' risk profiles are more similar to those in the male leader group than the women's. They are Upstagers, Rule Breakers, and Egotists. Therefore, even during conflict or difficult situations, they fight for resources, speak their minds, and will go against convention to succeed.

Corporate executive women share a mixed risk profile. They share a high Upstager score with the men's leader group and the CEO women's group. They have a moderately high Worrier score, although it is their high Upstager score that helps them stay engaged and asserting themselves even during tough discussions. They *Move Against* or may use aggression under stress and during conflict. They fight without backing down and continue to assert their views and ideas at all costs. This helps them stay in the limelight for higher leadership posts.

#4 — Perceptions Are Often Wrong and Much Tougher on Women

Perceptions and cultural biases are not only present but are often misguided as well as significantly more damaging to women.

We found that the perceptions about gender are considerably worse for women than most people think based on a comparison of our personality data and the Pew Cultural Survey. We found a real divide between the personality traits of women versus the related perceptions of those behaviors. We learned that frequently men and women leaders had personality scores that were parallel, yet the perceptions from the Pew Cultural Survey were severely harsh or negative towards women for the same trait or characteristic that was not considered negative in men.

#5 — Western European 2018 Study: Personality Risk Factor Study Confirms Worrier Trends in Women

The Western European study included 438 leaders and executives who were IE Business School participants. Of this group, there were 145 women leaders—six were executive women. There were 264 men leaders and 29 executive men in this study for a total of 293. While the sample size of the executive women's group is small (N=6), we viewed it as a trend and compared it to trends of executive/CEO women in our original North American studies. The highest risk for the women leaders was as Worrier with a 75% overall average, which was even higher than the women leaders' group in North America, so this is a significant issue holding women leaders back in Western Europe.

The IE women executives had a moderately high Worrier score, but had higher averaged scores as Rule Breaker, Upstager, and Hyper-Moody. Again, similar to the North American executive women and CEO study groups, these Western European executive women had more aggressive profiles than the women (non-executive) leader groups.

The men leaders in the Western European group were not similar to the North American men leaders' group. Their highest risks were

Detached, followed by Hyper-Moody, Cynic, then Worrier. So, for the most part, these men had *Moving Away* risk factors.

Lastly, the Western European men executives' (n=29) highest risk was Cynic, which is a *Moving Away* risk factor. Their next highest trends were Rule Breaker, Worrier, Eccentric, Detached, and Upstager. These executive men had a mix of both *Moving Away* and *Moving Against* risk trends.

#6 — Executive Women's Relationship-Building Skills: A Key to Their Success!

In CDR's research, corporate executive women had significantly higher Interpersonal Sensitivity scores on the CDR Character Assessment, which provides them with great relationship-building and networking skills. This helps them navigate to higher levels and win perception battles, succeed and thrive within the political structures of the organization, and build effective teams, networking, serving as talent coaches and mentors, and honing in on the needs and concerns of their stakeholders, including direct reports.

The good news for leadership effectiveness is that, unlike the men leaders and CEO women, corporate executive women's groups have lower Egotist scores.

The Crux of the Problem

There are clear expectations that leaders do not, and should not, run away or back down from tough issues or conflict. The missing part, up to this point, to understanding why the glass ceiling exists has been the unrecognized reality that women leaders go into Worrier behaviors. This undermines their upward progress as leaders because they are judged as lacking courage and confidence.

Men's Risks Are Viewed as More "Leader-Like"

The essential point is that the men, in greater numbers, are *Moving Against*—fighting for resources and airtime and aggressively winning the day, albeit with excessive, forceful, and "brave" tendencies. Men win the perception battle by having the stamina to stay in the game and fight to the end, while women run away, study, and analyze some more. Under pressure, more women tend to be cautious decision makers and to slow down the process. Men push forward with speed and force. Clearly, these overconfident and aggressive behaviors, which are exhibited more by men leaders, particularly as shown in our North American study group, are viewed as leader-like by the promotional power brokers.

Women Pulling Themselves Out of the Running

The existence of the glass ceiling is evidence that these risks are detrimental to women's success. When under pressure, many women default to self-defeating, diminishing behaviors—*ineffective coping strategies that take them out of the running for leadership positions.*

Women need to help each other stop resorting to these natural self-defeating and self-doubting tendencies and learn ways to manage, neutralize, and prevent Worrier behaviors from derailing their visibility, upward mobility, and success. One way to facilitate development is with individual assessment and coaching to help women (and men) understand and manage their own risks—particularly the Worrier tendency—more productively.

Chapters 9–12 provide insights, suggestions and even templates for women to develop their leadership capabilities, particularly if they are Worriers. Chapters 11 and 12 provide a roadmap to developing strengths, risk factors, and motivation to become highly effective leaders.

Takeaway from the Book *Lean In*

Sheryl Sandberg is a successful executive from Facebook and author of the popular book *Lean In: Women, Work, and the Will to Lead.* In *Lean In*, she describes herself as a classic Worrier and shares how she has learned to conquer, or at least quell, her fears and self-doubt:

> In order to continue to grow and challenge myself, I have to believe in my own abilities. I still face situations that I fear are beyond my capabilities. I still have days when I feel like a fraud. And I still sometimes find myself spoken over and discounted

while men sitting next to me are not. But now I know how to take a deep breath and keep my hand up. I have learned to sit at the table.[44]

Ms. Sandberg is keenly self-aware and has developed ways to manage and neutralize her tendencies toward worrying and fearfulness. Aspiring women leaders who have this Worrier trait can do the same. While training or wishing cannot erase this risk factor because it is an inherent reaction, carefully thought out and practiced developmental tactics can go a long way in managing, neutralizing, or preventing risk behaviors so they do not take women away from the table.

In addition, executives need to understand the ways many women tend to cope—and to be partners in helping those women learn more productive ways to deal with conflict and stress. Executives need to refrain from being overly jaded about a woman's tendency to worry because this frequently results in a fatalistic or stalled career trajectory for her. We saw in the studies cited in Chapter 4 that women often outperform when in leadership roles. Women have amazing talent, knowledge, and skills as leaders—and in all career vocations—so it is time we begin to appreciate their true capability.

We must also understand that all leaders and people, regardless of gender, have risk factors that result in ineffective or inappropriate behaviors. All risk factors have detrimental or erosive impact on performance. Therefore, everyone needs to become more self-aware and to build strategies to prevent damaging behaviors.

How 360° Leader Scan™ Feedback Describes Risk Factors Impacting the Glass Ceiling

Below are sample quotes from actual 360° Leader Scan™ performance feedback reports of leaders who have high risk factors in the scales highlighted in our glass ceiling study. The stakeholder comments below offer clear examples of how behaviors manifest for leaders who have the respective risks. Which behaviors are tolerated more readily or viewed as being more *natural* for leaders?

Worrier
- "Driven to achieve and works very hard. Unfortunately, not highly productive."
- "Needs to work at resolving problems faster."
- "Asks for too much information on all subjects."
- "Very indecisive, changes her mind too much."
- "Not seen as change oriented or as challenging the status quo, has very high standards, needs to anticipate issues in advance."
- "Inconsistent confidence level appears to others to be less than secure; however, is very capable and doesn't need to spend wasted energy concerned about how abilities are being interpreted by others."

Rule Breaker
- "He is seen as a person who puts seasonal sporting events above his relationship with the staff and his job."
- "He's a serial plagiarist."
- "I have seen her do some rather impulsive things, like sneaking into other people's confidential files."
- "He's had a number of people work under him over the years and most, if not all, have had trouble with him before leaving or asking to be reassigned."
- "I don't think anyone under him has respect for him or his work."

Egotist
- "Too often, people feel as though they are his "minions" doing the dirty work while he takes the credit."
- "She tends to belittle the people that interact with her by appearing to be flawless in her execution of assignments and by shifting blame when mistakes are made."
- "Takes credit for work done by an entire team of workers and does not acknowledge others for their extra effort."
- "Admission of mistakes does not happen."
- "Low level of self-awareness in terms of how his approach negatively impacts others."
- "Has a hard time working with others on the team as equals. He lets it be known that he has 'arrived,' while they 'still have a long way to go.'"

- "Has a hard time managing people 'underneath' her. Often demeans and is condescending. Doesn't show the proper respect to people around him."
- "Demands rather than delegates."

Upstager

- "Suggest [cultivating] politeness and manners; needs to avoid rude interruptions."
- "He consistently talks over people at company meetings."
- "Takes calls during conversations. Interrupts when information is being given."
- "She does not listen well, and it is hard to build any relationship with her."
- "Is highly defensive and often loses a powerful message in his defensiveness."

SEVEN

Why Are Risks So Important?

*"We're inclined to excuse in ourselves behavior
that we find unacceptable in others."*

—*Nido R. Qubein*

Risks are not aspects of our personality that we can just wish away or pretend don't exist—they are hardwired in us. They manifest when we feel uncomfortable and stressed, and when faced with pressure or conflict. The dilemma is this: Because our risks have become ingrained behaviors over our lifetime as natural responses to certain stimuli, we seldom recognize them. We may understand in the moment that we are not at our best, but frequently we do not realize how we are undermining our own effectiveness. Therefore, when our risks are left to run unchecked, we can hurt ourselves, our teams, and our clients, without realizing or intending to do so.

Because most people are unaware of their risks, those risks are constantly manifesting at work and at home, which can and does result in derailment––leadership derailment or, in the case of far too many women, the derailment of upward career mobility.

Risks and Derailers

There are a few assessments available that measure personality-based risk factors or that report on behaviors under stress. As mentioned previously, Kim and I developed and launched the CDR Risk Assessment as part of the CDR 3-D Suite in 1998.

> Designed to provide developmental feedback based on one's leadership risk assessment results. This report focuses upon 11 specific risk factors that are linked to 'universal leadership derailers,' that can potentially end, limit, or have substantial negative impact on leadership success. Another way to think about this information is to consider these risk factors as the 'dark sides' of your personality. These dark sides reveal themselves over time (i.e., once the honeymoon is over) and are especially evident under times of stress.
>
> The risk assessment scored results are based upon a scientifically validated psychological assessment tool that measures the occupational and organizational risk factors of normal personality. The normative data from which the CDR Risk Assessment Report results are generated consist entirely of working adults, not students or clinical patients.[45]

When we developed the CDR Risk Assessment, we also studied causes for leader "derailers" in an extensive literary review and developed the "8 Universal Derailers." These are included in the assessment report and linked to the "11 Risk Factors." For example, for Worriers, their likely derailers are that they

- are not decisive,
- seem to lack courage, and
- fail to adapt to changing demands.

8 Universal Leadership Derailers

Leadership success and (career) derailment largely depend upon two factors: 1) your relationships with others, including their perceptions about your performance; and 2) your contributions or results produced for the good of the organization.

Overwhelmingly, the first of these is the most critical in terms of leadership derailment. A leader may have produced outstanding results, yet if he or she has damaged relationships along the way or has operated with a lack of integrity, derailment may be inevitable. Universally, or across organizations, leadership derailers are defined below.[46] Dr. Leveridge and I developed the derailers taxonomy in 1998 after an exhaustive literary review.

Leadership success and derailment largely depend upon two factors:

1. How others perceive your performance, which includes your relationship with them

2. The contributions or results you've produced for the good of the organization

TABLE 3
Universal Leadership Derailers

HOW OTHERS PERCEIVE YOU:	YOUR POTENTIAL DERAILER IS:	RISK FACTORS:
Lack integrity; lack credibility; over-focus on personal agenda; fail to meet commitments	Erosion or betrayal of trust	False Advocate Rule Breaker Egotist Hyper-Moody Eccentric
Are slow to act; study issues and solutions too long; wait for instruction; are short on results	Failure to deliver and be accountable	Pleaser Rule Breaker False Advocate Egotist
Resist change; have difficulty with multiple priorities; lack flexibility	Failure to adapt	Perfectionist Worrier Cynic
Are risk aversive; freeze under uncertainty; fail to assert views; avoid making decisions	Lack of courage and decisiveness	Worrier Pleaser Perfectionist
Fail to support; have inappropriate emotionality or lack of "emotional intelligence"; create hostile work environment	Creating or endorsing a dysfunctional work environment	Egotist False Advocate Rule Breaker Cynic Hyper-Moody

Table 3 continues on the next page.

TABLE 3 (CONTINUED)
Universal Leadership Derailers

HOW OTHERS PERCEIVE YOU:	YOUR POTENTIAL DERAILER IS:	RISK FACTORS:
Fail to coach, mentor others, or provide developmental resources; are unconcerned with bench strength, organizational growth planning issues	Failure to develop people and organization	Egotist Worrier Cynic Detached
Lack a vision; cannot rally troops to produce; do not build enthusiasm toward stretch goals	Lack forward-looking and inspirational approach	Cynic Perfectionist Worrier
Have narrow views; undervalue diversity; strive to preserve personal wishes and biases; do not treat others fairly; do nt consider sufficient views or sufficient data in decision making	Lack objectivity and broad-mindedness	Egotist False Advocate Rule Breaker Upstager

SOURCE: Nancy Parsons and Kimberly Leveridge, PhD, CDR Assessment Group, Inc., 1998.

Examples of 11 Risk Behaviors

Below are examples of behaviors typical of the risk factors.[47] Note: these are actual examples from individual 360° reports that were used for leadership feedback coaching. Keep in mind, risks do not manifest the same for all people.

More Common with Women:

WORRIER – Stonewalls or fails to make timely decisions, performs unnecessary non-value-added tasks just to appease personal comfort level, over studies, is slow to act, and too risk aversive.

More Common with Men (North America):

RULE BREAKER – Fails to comply with safety rules, spends more funds than expenditure authority may permit, accesses confidential information from a coworker's computer, and skinny-dips at a company-sponsored function.

EGOTIST – Puts personal agenda ahead of the needs of the team, refuses to admit mistakes or pay attention to feedback, tends to think he/she is smarter or superior, takes credit for others' work, and behaves like a dictator or pompous member of royalty.

UPSTAGER – Misses social cues, pushes a passionate point of view too hard on the wrong people, talks over others, and does not let others take center stage.

The Additional 7 Risks Measured:

FALSE ADVOCATE – Seems to be agreeable while disagreeing internally—then goes against the decision or drags feet afterwards, says one thing and does another, nods head yes but actions later signal disagreement, and fails to live up to commitments.

CYNIC – Resists innovation with statements like "We have always done it this way," or "It'll never work," communicates doubt and pessimism about the business's future or projects, asks too many questions—often with a negative tone—and lacks trust in others to perform independently.

PERFECTIONIST – Keeps control by monitoring process details unnecessarily, requires too many updates from associates on work progress, and nitpicks errors instead of welcoming new concepts, ideas, or solutions.

PLEASER – Acts as an order-taker who needs to be told what to do, fails to defend their team's position, helps to a fault and can be easily exploited, and focuses more on the relationship with the boss than with associates or peers.

HYPER-MOODY – Shows a rollercoaster of emotions when pressed with changing priorities, yelling one minute then charming someone the next, and creates a tenuous environment where associates have no idea what temperament to expect next.

DETACHED – Fails to speak up at meetings (with a tendency to fade into the wallpaper), maintains minimal or distant relationships with associates, and shows reluctance to become involved in group dynamics.

ECCENTRIC – Dresses or behaves in non-conforming ways, alienates customers with bizarre or off-the-wall remarks, and makes statements from "left field." (Actual comments from high scorers: "I can feel my molecules moving," "We are looking for a house where there are trees and birds and where we can hear the earth breathe," and "I have so many ideas I sometimes feel like I have lotto balls in my head.")

The Most Important Step for Leadership Effectiveness Is to Identify Risks

The most important aspect of dealing with risk factors is *identifying* them. Once we know what our risk tendencies are, we can then begin to

1. Understand what triggers them—who (person, role, authority) and what circumstances cause the behavior to present (when I am confronted without fair warning, when my peer pushes my buttons, when people aren't prepared, etc.)

2. Think of when they manifest most often (when I am tired, angry, tense, when "Bob" shows up, when I am fearful, when there is controversy, etc.)

3. Identify what the impact of the behavior has been on self and others:

   - I offended someone and now have **damaged the trust and am off the team.**

   - My aggressiveness alienated my team and **they are now avoiding me.**

   - When I blurted out a response **it was clear I lost us the deal.**

   - My fear of speaking up resulted in **us losing XXX dollars on the project.**

   - My silence caused me **to lose visibility (hurting my promotability).**

   - When I did not openly provide needed feedback to help the employee improve, **the employee ended up being terminated, which could have been avoided.**

   - My negativity resulted in **derailing a new and better innovative design by the team.**

   - I took too much credit for the project and **now I am being excluded by the team.**

   - Because I didn't push back when I should have, **I am buried in work.**

- Or, impacts like **turnover, mistakes, team dysfunction, communications barriers, lackluster performance, opportunities lost, loss of respect, being too cautious and slow to act, and more**.

4. Most importantly, explore what one can do to prevent, neutralize, or manage these specific risks more effectively.

Chapter 12 provides a step-by-step approach to analyze and develop one's risk factors.

Why Leader Risks Are Not an Excuse for Bad Behaviors

While all leaders have their own array of inherent risk factors, some that result in inappropriate and dysfunctional behaviors, these personality predispositions are not an excuse for bad leader behaviors. Some of the risk behaviors like Worrier can be more detrimental to a person's career success; however, other risks, particularly *Moving Against* risks such as Egotist, Rule Breaker, Upstager, and Cynic, can cause harm or damage to others.

At CDR, we have coached thousands of executives around the globe. After the deep self-awareness assessment and coaching, only a few of these leaders have dug in their heels and said something like,

> *'Well, that is who I am . . . and my people will just need to deal with it.'*

The time has come to deal with unacceptable leader behaviors—through accountability and by no longer tolerating disrespectful behavior. For centuries leading up to today, too many leaders have been allowed to express, or have even been promoted for, their "bad" behaviors. Their bosses and boards just look the other way because of the bottom line or other results they enjoy.

This can and must stop. Effective leaders' primary job is to show their employees that they value and respect them. When leaders value their employees and stakeholders, they show them respect and support, cultivate their talent, and build trust to fortify healthy working relationships. This increases the odds for exceptional performance and loyalty.

Here's the catch: every leader has risks. And the fact is that every leader needs to manage his or her risks. Here are 10 suggestions for leaders to manage, neutralize, and prevent risks:

1. Take a deep dive assessment, including personality character traits/strengths, and a leadership risk assessment for derailment. I also advise a motivational assessment to learn one's intrinsic driver and reward needs.

2. Hire a leadership coach or assessment certified consultant to debrief and discuss your risks, what triggers them, and ways to manage and prevent them. *(We have many we can recommend!)*

3. Analyze your risks further, develop tactics and skills, and practice new approaches.

4. Work with a coach, mentor, or trusted advisor on an ongoing basis to work through your risks.

5. Manage your stress and your emotional responses to prevent automatically going to a risk response. Develop "in the moment" tactics to calm down or stabilize your emotional response.

6. Do work you enjoy and find captivating—when you are happy and content, your risks don't show.

7. Always be respectful and civil. *Always.*

8. Work with your team to share your risks and learn about theirs. Help each other.

9. If you misstep, apologize right away. Discuss and work on repairing the trust and building the relationship. Be vulnerable. Be humble.

10. Build on your new level of self-awareness. Build on your strengths, find hidden talents, work on those things you enjoy and that energize you. Know your risks and what triggers them—and manage them. Be accountable.

When a leader (intentionally) keeps his or her risks in check and shows people that he or she respects and values them, the sky is the limit. When a leader values people and builds trust, this has the power to transform the work environment from one of fear and misery to one of joy and fulfillment, where boundless achievements are possible.

EIGHT

Risk Connections and Clusters

"Invisible threads are the strongest ties."
—*Friedrich Nietzsche*

Everyone has his or her unique personality blueprint or puzzle pieces of traits that are connected. People are not simple, and neither are their array of personality strengths and risk factors. Sometimes a risk is opposite of a strength; other times risks are not connected in any way to a given character strength. We commonly hear that an overdone strength is usually a weakness, but that is not always the case when it comes to risk factors.

For example, usually if a man has very high Sociability on the CDR Character Assessment, he will also have a high score as an Upstager on the Risk Assessment. However, many women won't have this common configuration. They may have high Sociability, yet under their risks may be a Worrier. This plays out as a woman who is assertive and expressive when she is in her comfort zone and at her best. However, when her buttons are pushed or conflict occurs, she may clam up and go inside her head to analyze and freeze in fear. This, in turn, stops her from communicating as effectively as she does when she feels relaxed and not pressured. This is when—if she is wanting more visibility to advance her career—she actually grows more invisible when there is stress or adversity. Decision makers will almost automatically begin to assume or judge her to be a non-leaderlike candidate.

More commonly, however, people with high scores in Sociability traits go on talking and shift to their Upstager risk when they are facing conflict or pressure. Thus, they will hog the airtime and fervently push their points of view, often alienating or annoying others.

The CDR Character Assessment scores, or personality strengths, can also have an impact on how a specific risk factor will manifest. For example, if an individual has a very high score on Interpersonal Sensitivity, this usually softens how the Egotist risk factor will manifest for them. In the case where a leader has low Interpersonal Sensitivity with a high risk as an Egotist, this person could easily act in intimidating ways that can be perceived as disrespectful—or in ways that are forms of bullying. On the other hand, the high Interpersonal Sensitive Egotist will likely be warmer with people, yet make over-the-top comments about their own superior capabilities or intellect while remaining polite.

Ineffective Coping Strategies or "Risk Clusters"

Most people have clusters of *ineffective coping strategies*. For development, this helps put them into connecting themes making them less daunting to focus on.

Risk factors are often obstacles to an individual's overall effectiveness and thus can impede one's ability to get along and get ahead. Self-defeating behaviors have been studied by interpersonal theorists for seven decades. In 1945, psychoanalyst Karen Horney identified what we now refer to as ineffective coping strategies that can be summarized in terms of three themes:[48]

1. *Moving Away* – withdraws from others to achieve self-sufficiency and protection from interpersonal confrontations
2. *Moving Against* – uses aggressiveness and hostility to achieve power and personal admiration
3. *Moving Toward* – goes along with people in order to receive approval and affection

Horney's work set the stage for the study of dysfunctional dispositions and behavior in the workplace many decades later.

In part one of the CDR study, the women tended to react to adversity by *Moving Away* (Worriers). Both men and women executives tended to *Move Against*. From a leadership context, these ineffective coping strategies manifest as

- *Moving Away* – detaches, works behind the walls of office, goes silent, holds back, isolates, or just spirals into deep thought and analysis (**Worrier**, Detached, Hyper-Moody, Cynic, and False Advocate risk factors)
- *Moving Against* – becomes aggressive, pushy, stubborn, intimidating, and loud; will control airtime, uses a "my way or the highway" approach, or fights hard to win the day (**Upstager**, **Egotist**, **Rule Breaker**, and Eccentric risk factors)
- *Moving Toward* – seeks to smooth things over, becomes overly ingratiating, helps to a fault, becomes a "yes" person, takes on too much to make things better, or becomes unwilling to rock the boat or to challenge others (Perfectionist, Pleaser risk factors)

Illustration 2 shows the risk factors that are commonly associated with the *Moving Away, Moving Against,* and *Moving Toward* profiles.

ILLUSTRATION 2
Risk Assessment Clusters

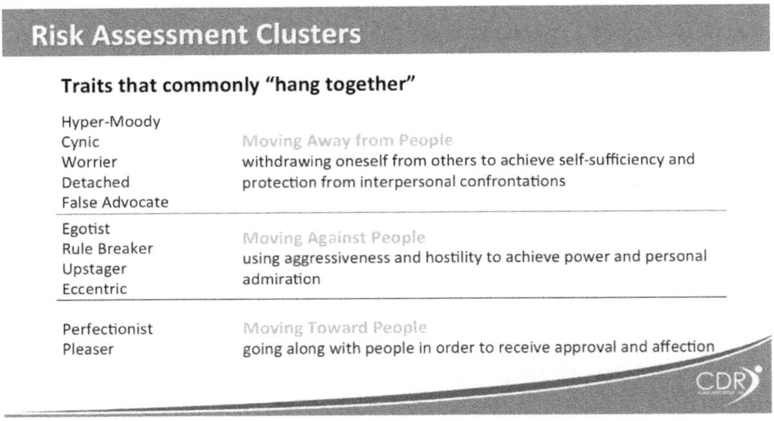

Risk Assessment Clusters

Traits that commonly "hang together"

Hyper-Moody	
Cynic	Moving Away from People
Worrier	withdrawing oneself from others to achieve self-sufficiency and
Detached	protection from interpersonal confrontations
False Advocate	
Egotist	
Rule Breaker	Moving Against People
Upstager	using aggressiveness and hostility to achieve power and personal
Eccentric	admiration
Perfectionist	Moving Toward People
Pleaser	going along with people in order to receive approval and affection

CDR

SOURCE: Nancy Parsons and Kimberly Leveridge, PhD, CDR Assessment Group, Inc., 1998.

Below are coaching and development tips for beginning to constructively address one's ineffective coping strategies and to improve confidence, performance, communications, upward mobility, and relationships. Chapter 12 provides detailed developmental ideas for each risk factor.

Understanding Those Who *"Move Away"*

Leaders and professionals who tend to be more technically and financially inclined, as well as many women, usually suffer most with *Moving Away* tendencies. Since many are Worriers, they clam up under pressure, holding back rather than injecting needed commentary and views. They close their doors, seek solitude, and often push themselves to work harder. They study and seek privacy versus jumping into a passionate dialogue or debate.

In 2018, as noted previously, we learned that the men leaders in the Western European study had some *Moving Away* traits with Detached as a key risk, whereas the European women were extremely high as Worriers. The men executives also had some *Moving Against* tendencies but not as profound as we found with the North America study of men leaders.

The performance problem that results from a team having *Moving Away* traits is that team members do not openly discuss the difficult issues or challenges together in order to come to the best solutions. Issues often remain avoided and unclear. Everyone stays inside his or her own head. This stress reaction of isolating oneself solidifies the separations that already likely exist. Imagine how these teams could thrive and push forward more quickly if key leaders and teams stayed at the table to discuss the challenging issues and opportunities more openly.

Developing the *"Moving Against"* Leader

Many books have been written on coaching and developing leaders who have a *Moving Against* profile. These can be the bullies and narcissists—the pushy, overly aggressive, stubborn, argumentative, negative, and intimidating types. This is very common in leadership because roughly 70% of leaders today have some level of propensity for the Egotist risk. Men and women CEOs in our North America study groups tended to have *Moving Against* profiles.

The *Moving Against* profile is that of an individual who jumps into a fighting and argumentative mode when his or her buttons are pushed.

Leaders and professionals who *Move Against* benefit by hiring a coach who will be assertive, confident, and comfortable holding a mirror to the client's behaviors so they may recognize the effect. Learning how to control the emotions, slowing down reactions, and finding tactful and appropriate ways to express dissent are all important developmental avenues for the *Moving Against* individual. Accountability for behaviors within organizations is most important for this type of behavior. It is unacceptable to intimidate or excoriate team members and direct reports. Despite passion levels, showing respect for all is non-negotiable.

Understanding Those Who *"Move Toward"*

Leaders who *Move Toward* and seek affection to smooth things over often lose the respect of others. They are frequently viewed as gutless, or as those who won't stand up and fight for others, particularly when it comes to their direct reports. They may get bypassed for promotions for being overly ingratiating or agreeable. Because they constantly volunteer to take on extra work out of fear of saying "no," they oftentimes are the ones who struggle with excessive work with no time to spare. The *Moving Toward* risks measured by the CDR Risk Assessment are Pleasers and Perfectionists.

Executive assistants and administrative personnel often share both of these risk factors. Fundamentally, *Moving Toward* people suffer from wanting to be "good boys" or "good girls," meaning they grew up being overly helpful and trying to be perfect. They want to please everyone. In their minds, they hope that if they only dig in and do more and do a perfect job, conflict and dissatisfaction will disappear. They especially want to satisfy and dote on authority figures.

From my 20+ years of executive coaching, the *Moving Toward* coping response is probably the most difficult and career-debilitating coping strategy for aspiring leaders.

However, this coping response is not hurtful or too damaging to those in certain professional roles such as executive assistants, dental assistants, nurse's aides, appointment schedulers, teacher's aides, tour guides, and similar occupations. Accountants, analysts, nurses, teachers, professors, reservation clerks, and others may have some of this coping response as well and still have solid performance, but they may need to manage these traits so they do not go too far and interfere with their effectiveness.

Developmental suggestions for the *Moving Toward* profile include hiring an objective, candid, and very patient executive coach who uses appropriate diagnostic assessments. Then, assertiveness training tops the list of recommendations for the Pleaser.

The Perfectionist, often part of the *Moving Toward* trends, needs to learn to back off from his or her compulsive need for control, for order, and to impose their personal standards. Extreme Perfectionists frequently have the deeper-rooted issue of obsessive-compulsive disorder (OCD) for which therapy may be helpful. Getting a Perfectionist leader to pull back, relax, and look beyond the nagging details is a steep challenge for even the most experienced coaches.

I now encourage Perfectionists to find executive coaches who have been successful in managing their own Perfectionist tendencies and to learn from them. From my coaching perspective, this is a daunting risk factor to successfully coach because of the Perfectionist's inherent compulsion to get it right to the smallest degree. Having them loosen up is contrary to their comfort zone and natural approach, so it is usually a longer-term developmental commitment. That is where a patient and persistent executive coach can help.

NINE

Advice and Stories
from Women Executives
and Leaders

*"Courage starts with showing up and
letting ourselves be seen."*

—*Brené Brown,* Daring Greatly

Advice from Women Executives

Interestingly, as we searched our research database for women leaders who were Worriers and who had risen to senior executive positions, they were few and far between. We only identified a handful, and three agreed to respond to our interview questions about how they managed to make it to the top despite this hefty risk factor. These executive women have all had coaching with their own CDR 3-D Suite results. Throughout their careers, they were self-aware and developed effective tactics to not permit their Worrier risks to sabotage their leadership success. Here are their stories and insights.

KAREN

COO of a large, nationally recognized Early Childhood Program and former VP of sales/marketing in the food manufacturing industry, serving several years running manufacturing plants in China

What has been the key to your success?

I am very calm under pressure and rarely lose my cool. I have come to appreciate the differing gifts that employees bring to the workplace, and to value their unique strengths, perspective, and energy for the work. There is truly not one right way to do things, and it's much more fun and engaging to lean in and be open to new approaches. I believe that relationships are the cornerstone of a successful workplace culture, and I strive to make a personal connection with everyone around me.

What is the greatest obstacle or personal development area you had to overcome in order to move up in the organization?

I'm an introvert by nature and have been told over the years that I can come across as aloof and unapproachable. My greatest challenge as an executive has been to become more comfortable engaging spontaneously with employees and clients in order to put people at ease and break down the power barrier. I've learned to regulate my tone and body language in an effort to convey more warmth, sincerity, and openness. I've even grown comfortable with putting on silly headbands with reindeer antlers or elf ears when handing out holiday gifts so employees know that I don't take myself too seriously!

How have you managed to keep the Worrier risk factor from impeding your success?

I have developed strong relationships with my direct reports and have confidence in all of them to make good decisions. I view my role as having the advantage of being able to see across the organization and work to limit my questions and feedback from that overview perspective, rather than delving into the weeds and micromanaging. I am very sensitive to not asking people to perform unnecessary, non-value added tasks, and encourage others to challenge me if a request doesn't make sense or seems unnecessarily onerous for their team. My relatively high Prudence and low Inquisitive scores serve as a counterbalance to my Worrier risk factor—put simply, I like to get things done and move on!

Knowing that many women in the leadership succession pipeline have Worrier as a primary risk factor when facing adversity or stress, what recommendations do you have for them to manage or neutralize this risk factor?

Self-care is the key! I keep my anxiety and high-stress levels in check by taking care of my health and well-being—eating well, exercising often, reading for pleasure, connecting with loved ones, and practicing mindfulness. It took me a long time to realize that these elements must become the essence of daily life—they are not the things one gets around to after the work is done!

NICOLE

A national managing partner in a top, global, financial consulting firm who heads up her firm's "People Experience"

What has been the key to your success?

I believe the key to my success has been grit, non-linear think-ing, and being open to possibilities. Often women work just as hard or harder than men but don't get ahead. Yet they feel that they can be advanced because of their hard work or work eth-ic, though this is often not the case. I think "grit" adds another dimension to that where you demonstrate a very strong work ethic but do it strategically to be able to show your impact and seek out ways to make that known and visible. I also am a non-linear thinker in a world of other CPAs and consultants who tend to be very linear thinkers. I see the possibilities and the big picture when others don't and am able to synthesize many points of view into one cohesive point of view and ac-tion plan. Throughout my career I have been open to pursuing non-traditional paths within my profession; this has allowed me to hone certain skills but also to demonstrate many key operational skills that weren't always evident in a traditional role.

What is the greatest obstacle or personal development area you had to overcome in order to move up in the organization?

The greatest obstacle I had to overcome was not being viewed as someone that was multi-dimensional. As an audit partner, you tend to be put in a box as far as people's perception of you without being given the opportunity to demonstrate an ability to show other key strengths. I have had to really advocate for myself in order to be given other opportunities to soar.

How have you managed to keep the Worrier risk actor from im-peding your success?

I am a woman of strong faith. I think I will always worry, but I know that ultimately when I am not in control of a situa-tion, all I can do is my best and then accept whatever outcome results. It took me a long time to get to that point. What has been my Worrier risk in the past has now morphed into being more of an "analyzer" trait in a positive way—where I tend to ask questions that challenge others to think differently and help us all as a team move forward.

Knowing that many women in the leadership succession pipeline have Worrier as a primary risk factor when facing adversity or stress, what recommendations do you have for them to manage or neutralize this risk factor?

Keep in mind what you can influence in your "20 square feet." Worriers often want to solve all the problems around them when many times the problem does not even directly affect them. I also think that Worriers need to be able to discern what things are "gravity" or just a product of their circumstances versus things that they can actually influence or control. I have a plaque on my desk that says, ***"Embrace the imperfections, the chaos, the holy mess of your beautiful life."*** I try to live by that mantra. *[Emphasis added on this quote!]*

ELAINE

PhD serves as CEO of a pharmaceutical and biotechnology firm specializing in early stage pharmaceutical development

What has been the key to your success?

Having a supportive community. Growing up, it never occurred to me that I couldn't do something, and I credit my mother with that attitude. But since then, I have curated a close network of individuals that have helped me in a variety of ways. Mentors and sponsors have guided me through uncharted waters and promoted me to their networks. Female friends and colleagues who can provide advice help me through imposter syndrome and commiserate (it is good to know that you are not alone)! And finally, I have a supportive spouse who not only listens and makes me laugh on those bad days, but who shoulders most of the household duties too.

What is the greatest obstacle or personal development area you had to overcome in order to move up in the organization?

Myself. I capped myself at COO. I didn't want to take the step to CEO. Frankly, it scared me. I didn't want the burden, and I didn't think I could do it. I preferred having that one more layer of "protection." As CEO, it can feel like everything rests on your shoulders. But when the board asked me to step into the role, I realized I wasn't alone. I had an excellent team and supportive board that wanted our company (and me) to succeed.

How have you managed to keep the Worrier risk factor from impeding your success?

I have worked on my issues with delaying tough decisions and stating my views with assertive team members. Some of those have been stemmed by growing more comfortable with my own knowledge and skill set and becoming more confident. And I have dealt with my "analysis paralysis" and learned that not every decision requires deep diligence and absolute perfection. I still struggle with approval-seeking for certain decisions but, being data driven, I started to track data (on myself and outcomes of my decisions and other organizations) to help remind me that I make good decisions and that I am in-line with others in my industry.

Knowing that many women in the leadership succession pipeline have Worrier as a primary risk f actor when facing adversity or stress, what recommendations do you have for them to manage or neutralize this risk factor?

One thing that hindered me is my lack of confidence. But that came from a feeling of having to know absolutely everything about everything. And that isn't what a CEO needs to do. I know what I am very good at and rely on my team to help in the other areas.

"Worrier" Stories and Struggles Shared by Women Leaders

Below, several women leaders share the challenges they routinely face as Worriers and the impact of their behaviors on their effectiveness, work-life balance, and success. (I first shared their stories in my book *Fresh Insights to END the Glass Ceiling.*)

ANN

CEO of Creative Services/Communications and Marketing Firm

One time I was brought into a complicated business issue with one of my business divisions. Thinking the worst, I brought the whole team down with my negative speculation and over-thinking. The team could sense my fear, and they all began to fear the situation as well. It turned out to be a simple solution with the client, and I felt like a fool. I saw that my fear harmed my team. My fear even caused one valuable team member to feel inadequate and concerned for her future with our company.

There are times I wake up at night and try to process business challenges, overthinking and overanalyzing to the point to where I cannot go back to sleep. Over and over . . . every night. I think it takes me longer to make decisions because of this fear-based operation in my head.

On the flip side, the Worrier in me has kept me from making some bad decisions and always keeps me on my toes. I am acutely aware of threats and challenges, and I certainly know how to dodge bullets. In some strange way, using my fear more productively has made me a stronger leader and has allowed me to grow a successful, sustainable business.

As a Worrier who leads people, I worry most about these three things: money, people, and business excellence. My business must have the right people working for the right people, make money, and do a good job every day. When any of these three is in jeopardy, I worry.

MELANIE

Executive Vice President, Energy Company

Even as an executive vice president, there have been times I should have given my opinion, knowing I was right, but I worried about how my opinion would be perceived if I did not have the time to prepare both my approach and tone. As a result, I missed the opportunity to demonstrate my leadership and competence and to openly contribute to important conversations of the senior leadership team.

DIANE

President, Women's Entrepreneurial Leadership Organization

I went back to complete my MBA more than 10 years after I got my bachelor's degree. I was a married adult student with a full-time job.

In one of my very first assignments after returning to school, we were asked to write a paper on a key business issue. I spent 40 hours preparing this paper over the following week. I worked until late at night (after getting off work) and over the weekend to get it done in time. I was worried about what the teacher expected of me and didn't want to fail.

After we turned in our papers, the teacher indicated that he had just expected us to spend a couple of hours completing the assignment.

As a working person, I had gone into hyperdrive because I was worried about getting a good grade on one paper (something that, in reality, would have had a minimal impact on my life or career, even if had been mediocre).

I have since gotten much better about determining expectations before embarking on a new project.

KATHY

Business Manager of Consulting Firm and Recent Director of Largest Division of Industrial Materials Manufacturer

As a Worrier, I had a tendency to always run my ideas past someone I trusted, first. I have worried about giving an incorrect example or sounding stupid, which would have been so humiliating.

I was the only female leader reporting to the executive vice president, yet I was the only direct report without the title of vice president. I believe my Worrier risk impacted how I was perceived and that is likely why I was not promoted to the vice president level.

Due to my risk as a Worrier, I would shut down in meetings with my superiors. I would do the same in meetings mixed with superiors and peers, paralyzed by self-doubt and a sense of inferiority. People within the organization became so familiar with my paralyzed, fearful behavior that they adjusted to me. They knew I often had solutions so would prompt me, or even worse, my boss would adjourn a meeting to listen to my ideas. He would then resume the meeting later to present my ideas or my solutions while I stayed quiet. So, essentially, everyone did a "work-around" with me due to my reputation of having overwhelming fear of speaking up in the group.

I unintentionally created a self-defeating, dysfunctional work environment that became the accepted "norm" by an entire division as a method of operation. With four hundred people under me, I wouldn't speak up to my boss and peers at a meeting due to my Worrier risk. (This reluctance to speak up to her boss was a combination of her Worrier traits along with her elevated risk score as a "Pleaser.")

Over the years, as a Worrier, I never thought I knew enough about a new subject, no matter how much experience I had; I always refrained from giving my thoughts freely; I always second-guessed my responses when someone challenged me, even when I knew I was right.

Interestingly, as the department head of the largest department in a North America division of an industrial materials manufacturing company, my Worrier traits never arose during meetings or challenges with my direct reports and staff in my own department.

The worrying tendencies also came at bedtime for me. I was clear, concise, and decisive at my staff meetings and could field as many questions and challenges as anyone could come up with; in fact, I welcomed it. However, if there was a major decision involved, I always had a contingency plan or nagging thought that arose during the night. This caused me to run and rerun different scenarios in my head and analyze the secondary plan down to the last detail.

I finally started keeping notecards available on my nightstand to write down thoughts and ideas during the night so that I could remind myself that I had already been through this, which allowed me to relax and go back to sleep.

JOANNE

A WORRIER AFTER THE FACT
Vice President, Marketing, Banking Industry

As a Worrier, I sometimes wake up at night and am not able to get a work issue from forming an endless loop in my head, preventing further sleep and any productive problem-solving. These are mostly big work issues that we all have, but can also be minor things that become huge frustrations.

My worrying tends to happen *after the fact* or after a decision is made. I'm actually THE change agent in my organization, the risk-taker (albeit within old-school banking culture with at least some calculation behind the risk); I speak up in meetings most frequently and make decisions quickly and confidently. If only reading about the description of a Worrier and resulting indicators, I would bypass it as something I didn't relate to and ignore the lessons to be learned that can indeed hold one back from furthering her career.

My particular indicators of a Worrier are more *after* the decisions have been quickly and confidently made. And, mostly at night when I should be getting restorative, problem-solving sleep! I've tried to develop good mental health techniques to sleep better—meditation and attention to good sleeping habits. I've even considered antianxiety medication, but haven't wanted to resort to that just yet.

On the bright side, I tend to have a Plan B for bigger projects, and I have to say Plan B has come in very handy on numerous occasions. I also think all this late-night worrying gives me more of a 360° vision than most. I can and do still make decisions quickly and confidently, but I think it's been honed over many years of quickly thinking about all sides of an issue and being able to spot potential pitfalls to avoid during execution. Perhaps, too, I've learned over the years that no one likes a naysayer, and I've developed methods to quickly identify where problems might be and then become part of the solution.

I've rambled on too long (don't recall but probably also had "elevated communication")! Then, again, I may be worrying over nothing!

BRENDA

AN ASPIRING FUTURE LEADER
Consulting Firm Intern and Industrial/Organizational Psychology Graduate Student

I overthink my emails. It takes me too long to find a response that I am comfortable with and that I think will be perceived the *right* way. If I send an important email and don't receive a somewhat prompt response, I begin to worry that the delayed response is due to my not using the right words to express my thoughts. However, in reality, people are just busy.

As a Worrier, when I filled out job and graduate school applications, I am pretty certain that I took twice the amount of time another person would have. I became fixated on little details about my responses and submission instructions that most likely go unnoticed by the selection committees. I also took extra steps, like researching how people have handled these applications in the past to make sure I was making the right decisions, so that I didn't jeopardize my chances of being accepted.

TEN

Top Executive Coaches Offer Advice for Women "Worriers"

"Awareness makes us emotionally brilliant."

—Lori Myers

Fortunately, there are many highly capable executive coaches today who help clients, including high-potential leaders, develop and grow. I strongly encourage those seeking executive coaching services to make sure that the coach they consider is using appropriate deep dive scientific assessments. They should be certified in using instruments beyond 360°s, MBTIs, or similar tools. Coaches who are certified in the coaching process alone may be beneficial to a limited extent. However, if coaches lack the scientific tools and the art of feedback, they may shortchange their clients.

Furthermore, if you hire a coach who does not use tools in the genre of the CDR 3-D Suite, you will spend a lot of time and money while only scratching the surface of your behaviors and will not be able to explore why behaviors manifest in the ways they do. Tools such as these are ideal for providing a clear reading on the difference between your intent and your impact.

I selected several of the best executive coaches I've worked with throughout the past two decades who have extensively used our assessments, particularly the CDR Risk Assessment, and asked them to provide developmental suggestions for women who are Worriers. Their suggestions follow.

CAROLYN MAUE

President, The Maue Center
Orlando, Florida
Email: carolyn@mauecenter.com

How have you helped women to overcome their Worrier risk behaviors?

I use a Leadership Development Coaching model, and included in it is an assessment process that includes the CDR Assessment, and often with executives, I will also conduct "360 Degree" interviews to get perceptions of the leader's strengths and opportunities for development from a cross-section of the leader's superiors, peers, and staff members. A core principle of my coaching is to build on the leader's strengths, helping him or her to utilize those strengths more often and in different ways, while mitigating weaknesses and/or risk behaviors.

I have helped female leaders overcome their risk behaviors by looking at how they can utilize their strengths more often. Some female leaders with whom I have worked have been very strong in Prudence, and we build on that to assist them in preparation. Other female leaders with whom I have worked in coaching have been very strong in Leadership Energy, Interpersonal Skills, and Sociability. These women have found that when they talked over their concerns with their staff, as well as engaged peers and team members in the challenge, their isolation and worry diminished.

What developmental suggestions do you have for women who are Worriers and who overanalyze, freeze, or go quiet out of fear of failure?

It is very important to be prepared, but for those who tend to overanalyze, this can be a danger zone. So, it is important to be prepared in a way that "opens up the windows and doors" and engages others in the preparedness. My experience with women leaders who are Worriers is that it worsens when they isolate, or when they do not use their strengths to feel confident. They can feel intimidated by those in the room who are louder or quicker. Therefore, preparation, and alignment with others in the room and others who know what the leader is trying to accomplish, is essential. So, the suggestions include the following:

1. Assure thorough preparedness, using your strengths, whether that be in prudence, interpersonal skills, etc.
2. Share the information with others and engage them in your ideas.
3. Prepare for all surprises, particularly ahead of meetings.
4. Engage an executive champion who understands your goals and where you want to go and who can provide advice and access to other resources in the organization.

Please share one of your best success stories in helping a woman leader to advance in her career.

A female leader with whom I worked had a PhD in research, had spent most of her life leading teams in labs, and now was responsible for both running a team, engaging peers across departments, and substantiating the need and funding for a multimillion dollar program in a large healthcare organization. She was basically doing three jobs at once—manager, director, and executive VP. It was at the executive level that she lacked confidence and where her "worry" emerged.

She was very strong in Prudence, and also Adjustment. So we focused on those strengths to help her as she prepared presentations for funders and decision makers, and she developed intricate and well-documented graphs and charts that conveyed the information. She also prepared herself well for these meetings and conveyed a sense of confidence and optimism due to her high Adjustment. She was very successful in getting the funding, and is now running a multimillion dollar state-of-the-art program in cutting-edge research.

How important is it for aspiring women to gain a clear understanding of their inherent strengths, risks, and intrinsic motivators for success?

It is the key to their success. All leaders must have a vision for themselves and they need to determine where they want to go. It is important to have a strong knowledge of their strengths and how to use them often, and have an ability to explain their strengths to others. Having knowledge of their risks and how to mitigate them is crucial for success. They should have self-awareness of their own drivers and values and about what motivates them. I believe every person/leader is distinct and unique and that when they have this self-awareness, they can then build their skills in managing and leading others, thereby building capacity in their teams, organizations, and communities. Most leaders have leadership skills that are like "Swiss cheese"—strong in some areas, absent in others—because in our organizations we don't have a consistent way of preparing leaders. Knowledge of one's own strengths, risks, and motivators is essential to filling these gaps and maximizing one's unique contributions as a leader.

What other advice do you have for aspiring women leaders?

It is very important that each leader has self-awareness and knowledge as described above. It is also very important to be part of a community of leaders. Our society gives out messages that we can "do it all." We usually can't do it all at once, and not alone. So, my advice is, along with self-knowledge and awareness, to become part of a community of female leaders with whom you can give and take knowledge, experience, and wisdom. Your community may include professional colleagues, other women in your organization, or a professional organization. Being connected to a larger community allows our richest talents to emerge.

MARIANNE ROY, Med, MS PCMH, PCC

Nationally Recognized Organization Development Consultant;
Executive Coach; Facilitator
Nashua, New Hampshire
Email: marianne@roy-associates.biz

(Marianne has been certified and using CDR Assessments for two decades.)

How have you helped women to overcome their Worrier risk behaviors?

- My first strategy is to help them understand that risk factors first developed as coping strategies when we were young–– they may have gotten us through the day at some point, but as adults it may not serve us so well.
- Next, I think it is important that women get to know their Worrier: What triggers it, how does it show up? What do they worry about? What is the impact? How has it served them? What is their Worrier costing them in terms of stress, career, family relationships, etc.?
- Once they truly 'get' the price they are paying, my clients will often say, "Enough, let's find a different way."

- Over the last couple of years, I have begun to incorporate CBT (Cognitive Behavioral Therapy) with good success. If she can understand the underlying beliefs that are leading to the worry, we can work on reframing.
- Experimenting with different strategies to turn the Worrier switch off or turn down the volume. Role-playing, mindfulness techniques, preventive strategies.

What developmental suggestions do you have for women who are Worriers and who overanalyze, freeze, or go quiet out of fear of failure?

- Meditation.
- Role-playing.
- CBT—*Feeling Good* by David Burns is excellent for the lay person—gives lots of concrete things to do.
- Doing small experiments and debriefing for learning vs. whether or not they were successful (e.g. arrive at the meeting a few minutes early, target one individual you are intimidated by, go up to them and say "hello" and ask a question). Debriefing entails asking these questions: How did it go? What was hard? What was easy? What did you learn? What is the next experiment?

  (The experiment has to be calibrated—it can't be too easy or too hard. Just enough so it pushes her out of her comfort zone, yet she has a good chance of succeeding with your support.)

Please share one of your best success stories in helping a women leader to advance in her career.

Amanda* is a high-ranking nurse practitioner in the National Health Service (NHS). She is the clinical manager of a large pediatric dental surgical center. At the time I was called in to work with her, she was in danger of being let go from the clinic (essentially unheard of in the military world). This would have had significant consequences for her career in the NHS. Her position would be difficult to fill, so there would also be significant consequences for this busy clinic.

*Name has been changed to protect confidentiality.

We did her CDR, and I did interviews—the equivalent of a 360°. The themes from the interviews were that Amanda was technically excellent, an efficiency machine, and no one wanted to work with her. She also had many complaints from parents about being insensitive and rude.

Her CDR revealed she had extremely low Interpersonal Sensitivity and high Prudence—specifically high Moralistic, high Perfection and Task Mastery, as well as Perfection as a risk factor. She came from a family background that valued science, precision, and efficiency.

The pediatric clinic she was working in had many staff and physicians who were warm and caring (what you would expect from those working with young children). The children the clinic worked with had many complex issues. Families would more often than not fly to the clinic and have to stay for several days after the procedure.

Honestly, in the beginning this felt like a "teaching a fish to fly" project. Because of the way the military system works (at her rank, she could not just take another job) she decided she wanted to try to make it work. I must admit that I was not optimistic at the beginning. However, at some point it dawned on me that while I couldn't "teach a fish to fly," I could teach a fish to fake flying. And that is exactly what we did. We put together checklists. Each morning she was to say "Good morning" to all the surgeons and staff she would work with that morning. First thing on Monday morning, she scheduled time to ask key individuals how their weekend was. She put birthdays in her calendar and would wish individuals a "Happy Birthday" on their special day.

She talked to doctors to find out their surgical preferences, and we worked out how she would accommodate their wants—even though it wasn't as efficient.

We worked out 'compassion' protocols for common parent situations. Questions for her to ask parents about preferences—even if it made things less efficient or she didn't agree with what they wanted.

Three years later, I got this message from her Colonel:

> I wanted to drop you a line and let you know how
> Amanda is doing. Since you worked with her, her doctors
> and other coworkers have become so attached to her that

they are going to allow her to telecommute so she can care for her ailing mother. Mary (her boss) said that she has had a huge turnaround, and they don't want to lose her— not because they can't find another nurse, but because they like Amanda so much.

BRIAN EPPERSON, PhD

Founder, Human Performance Advisors; Professor and Chair, Graduate Business Programs, Newman University
Tulsa, Oklahoma
Email: bepperson@humanperformanceadvisors.com

How have you helped women to overcome their Worrier risk behaviors?

I have always believed that the basis of worry (as well as confidence) is rooted in timidity and self-doubt regarding achievement of some task or aspiration. The academics call this "self-regard." We don't worry about things we have mastered and that are within our control. We worry about the things we don't feel competent in or are outside of our control.

I also firmly believe worry comes from a place rooted in the belief that failure and setbacks can actually be avoided. It is a logical inconsistency when individuals are striving to become great. Stretching equals failure. Forrest Carter once said, "Everything growing wild is a hundred times stronger than tame things." As in nature, what creates character, strength, or resilience has never been a product of the smooth and easy path of least resistance. It is a logical inconsistency. The career, aspiration, or achievement you so achingly imagine is never going to crystallize until you learn (or even love) to run into the crucible. The crucible is where the dabblers and amateurs choose their exits––the professionals learn to love the fire. I'd like to share this passage from Ryan Holiday, the author of *The Daily Stoic*:

George Ball, the diplomat and advisor to President Kennedy (one of whom David Halberstam would call 'the best and the brightest'), once observed about Lyndon Johnson that LBJ was hardly disadvantaged by his lack of an Ivy League education. Rather, he said, LBJ suffered from his sense of lacking that education. That is, LBJ's insecurity about his deficiency was far worse than any actual deficit that may have existed. . . . LBJ was convinced that he had been done an injustice by growing up poor and unable to afford a school like Harvard or Yale. On its face, this was absurd—he still ended up being President. . . . He was harmed by his lack of education. . . . because he harmed himself by believing there was something lacking.

What developmental suggestions do you have for women who are Worriers and who overanalyze, freeze, or go quiet out of fear of failure?

All battles are fought incrementally. I very often encourage compartmentalizing their days into twenty-four-hour blocks where absolute and total focus are given to the day they are engaged in. Capturing hills or climbing mountains is always less mentally taxing when the day's climb is all they are focused on. As it applies to worry, generically, worry is going to come. Nevertheless, external resources, such as other people, can be used to vet the level of worry to determine appropriate levels of worry. Second, giving themselves deadlines for engaging in or making a decision, thus reducing the amount of time given to unhealthy rumination.

Please share one of your best success stories in helping a women leader to advance in her career.

I worked with an immensely talented woman who had rocketed up the corporate ladder in a Fortune 500 company and, despite being young, had eclipsed her peers by two decades. She had the drive, the work ethic, and the intelligence to do well but simply did not have the right mental framework to deal with the added pressure of senior management or her belief in her own capabilities.

We worked to identify her belief systems that hindered progress. We also worked to identify truths and facts about "what was true" about her (she was not seeing herself accurately). As simple as it sounds, she began to review these truths (e.g., achievements, pedigree, timelines of promotion, successful tenure in management, etc.) on a daily, habitual basis. This was not like "Stuart Smalley" where you would feed the machine a bunch of positive mantras and sayings; it was data and facts that were true about her. Over a span of four months, I watched her transform into the executive she could be by simply turning off the valve of self-doubt and drenching her mind in what was simply already true about herself. Surprisingly, so many of us are our own worst enemies.

How important is it for aspiring women to gain a clear understanding of their inherent strengths, risks, and intrinsic motivators for success?

It is imperative. I have discovered, as has every other leader, that the things that hurt leaders the most are the things they cannot see. The developmental space is obsessed with strengths, and rightfully so, but what we often forget is that many women have immense strengths and talents that they don't see as such. The climb is a slippery one in corporate America, and the primary hurdles that must be transcended are the ones between their ears. A comprehensive understanding of themselves allows them to fully leverage the abilities they have, mitigate their risks, and determine not only why they are doing something––but most importantly, see just how far they could actually go if they gave themselves permission.

What other advice do you have for aspiring women leaders?

Simple: see how uncommon you can become in your space. It's harder work, it requires longer hours and higher expectations, but when the drive to surpass what is reasonable becomes the overarching driver, it is astonishing to see the transformation (and reward) that occurs in people. I believe—actually, I am utterly convinced—that we rarely, if ever, maximize our full potential. In short and in that vein, my advice is this: make it a goal or obsession to see exactly how far you can go, learn to embrace and welcome failure, and never stop trying to see how much potential is there. This will push the boundaries on our upper limits, creating higher highs and higher lows and this . . . becomes addictive!

BARBARA MINTZER MCMAHON, PCC, MCEC, MSW, MFT

Certified Executive Coach; Leadership Development Expert
San Francisco Bay Area
Email: thectm@moraga.net

How have you helped women to overcome their Worrier risk behaviors?

Let me start with an acknowledgement—I have a great deal of personal experience dealing with the Worrier Self. Truth be told, early in my marriage (almost 40 years to date), my husband gave me the official title of CWO (Chief Worry Officer). I know this role well. The good news is that I have been on a long learning journey to manage this role with increased mastery and have found a plethora of best practices that have changed the way I live and coach. I have found that life can be transformed in ways I didn't imagine through the practices of Mindfulness.

Why Mindfulness Matters: The foundation of mindfulness is "Awareness." It is about being aware of our internal and external environment. It is about building on connections, living with compassion, focusing on what has most meaning, and making conscious choice. Not always easy. However, important—especially for Women in Leadership who worry about

- meeting the needs of others,
- being perfect at everything all the time,
- making a wrong move—wrong choice—or
- missing an opportunity.

Let's start with Awareness. It is a choice. A choice we make multiple times a day, every day of our lives. Consciously or unconsciously we are deciding: Stay or Go? Life/work puts the unexpected in front of us, and we make decisions about whether to put our full attention to these moments or not. These moments are the turning path. These are the questions: Do you move toward what is most meaningful? Are you being purposeful? How will this impact your greater vision for what you value most?

Example

- You're working on a deadline, and your coworker comes to your office door and asks for a moment of your time. You must make a choice. Yes or No? Be there or not?
- You have a meeting to facilitate and your head is pounding and stomach churning. Take a moment or just head for the board room?
- Your boss tells you about an opportunity to present at a meeting next week across the country. Stay or Go?
- You're at home trying to follow up on business from work, and your kid comes into the room and wants to talk to you about what happened with a friend.
- You're trying to get sleep and you're distracted by the chatter in your worried mind.

To be fully present or not, in the good moments and the more challenging moments, is key. And, when we fail to take this challenge on, we abandon opportunity to pilot our own lives. This is a critical concern for women more often than men. As the research has proven, men are more likely to assume they have the right answer and are able to take an aggressive step into the unknown. Women, on the other hand, frequently doubt themselves and "freeze vs. forge." It is in these moments when mindfulness matters. Here are some practices I have found that can help.

Find Solitude: The research findings on women and what happens when we derail suggests that we can react to the Worrier Self by cutting off from others. This can happen in reaction to our own critical self (i.e. not feeling good enough or out of fear of getting hurt). We can withdraw and isolate. Which we recognize as the opposite of key competencies required for successful and sustainable leadership (decisiveness, collaboration, relationship management, and the ability to partner strategically). To create these strong reciprocal relationships, we must understand and be able to execute on individual strengths and be guided by our wiser self.

It requires truly knowing and honoring the self. Finding alone time is key. To allow time for deep listening and reflecting on your personal strengths, understanding what is most meaningful for your own sense of well-being and your capacity to perform. Remembering you can't save others without attending to self. Practices that can help in sustaining this connection include,

- time on the calendar to 'be' with yourself and reflect, and
- finding or creating the environment that will support this type of connection—to pause, breathe, listen, reflect, and re-engage with your best self.

Exercise Self-Compassion: Drop the judgement and befriend yourself. Practice extending the same kindness and compassion you would to a friend, direct report, or colleague in crisis. Pivot away from the path of Perfection and focus on being on Purpose. Ask yourself: What do I feel? What do I need? Is it 'critical' that this be Perfect? Remember the 80/20 rule, that 20% of your activities will account for 80% of your results.

Show Up: The good and bad news about the female brain is that many have the capacity to multi-track. It is akin to being Ringmaster for all seven circles in the circus. Not possible to teach/tame/oversee the animals in all seven rings. Recognize this and bring your attention to one ring. Stop, Breathe, Assess, and Choose to Attend to what is most important.

DANIEL FELDMAN, PhD

President, Leader Performance Solutions; Executive Coach
New York, NY
Email: dfeldman@leadershipperformance.com

How have you helped women to overcome their Worrier risk behaviors?

The first step is to help female leaders recognize that a Worrier profile doesn't necessarily arise out of a lack of capability or some personal flaw. This type of thinking can perpetuate indecisiveness and lack of confidence. Female leaders often feel the pressure of unfair scrutiny or unrealistic expectation. By objectively recognizing the challenge and perhaps lack of support that exists, you open the door to new approaches toward building greater self-confidence. I encourage women to examine a situation in a realistic way and to break down the challenge into smaller pieces.

What developmental suggestions do you have for women who are Worriers and who overanalyze, freeze, or go quiet out of fear of failure?

Courage is the judgment that something else is more important than fear. The goal is not to eliminate fear but to focus on your goal. I invite female clients to valiantly confront their problems and push beyond their comfort zone. Specific steps include the following:

- Recognize what you are afraid of and put it into perspective.
- Focus on the benefits of taking the risk.
- Tolerate the discomfort.
- Practice by envisioning the steps to success.

Please share one of your best success stories in helping a women leader to advance in her career.

I was coaching a senior director in a large, well-established engineering company. She was a millennial in a successful, stable, and conservative organization whose managerial ranks held a preponderance of older men. The management team sincerely supported the development of female leaders and was proactive in succession planning for the future. Still, my coaching client would run into unintended barriers and unconscious bias about how she was expected to act, present herself, and communicate, that at times made her dismayed and/or angry.

These barriers, and internal self-doubt, contributed to her becoming overly self-conscious and second guessing herself. Through our coaching work together, she dug deep to shine the light onto her own self-limiting thoughts and tendencies. She took on homework assignments to try out new ways of interacting that promoted a more assertive style. Ultimately, she built an executive presence that was uniquely her own, enhancing her impact and effectiveness.

How important is it for aspiring women to gain a clear understanding of their inherent strengths, risks, and intrinsic motivators for success?

First, gaining perspectives about yourself helps to identify your developmental opportunities and orient you towards growth. Women need to own their strengths fully, understand the tendencies that limit them, and enlist the energy of their personal drivers.

What other advice do you have for aspiring women leaders?

There has been a tremendous growth in supportive networks for women, formally and informally. I would encourage female leaders to seek out those connections and groups that best fit their lifestyle and discover the power in numbers.

LYNNE PRITCHARD

President, LCP Consulting; Executive Coach
Tulsa, Oklahoma
Email: lcpritchard@icloud.com

How have you helped women to overcome their Worrier risk behaviors?

I offer several techniques that have helped Worriers overcome these career-paralyzing behaviors:

1. *Set one time aside per day to worry.* Frequently, women worry and fret over the same issue multiple times per day. Whether it is revisiting the outcome of a past issue or visualizing all that can go wrong with a future issue—worrying is a major time waster—and, more importantly, erodes confidence. I advise Worriers to set aside a time of day to worry. Yes, just one time per day—maximum worry time allowed: 30 minutes. Make an appointment on your calendar to worry just as you would schedule time with a client. Stop once you start to repeat a worry and move onto something else more productive. Every time a worry comes into your head outside of this time, say to yourself,

"No. Stop. This is not a designated worry time." It takes some practice, but after some time people can gain some valuable time back by "worrying" only once per day.

2. *Keep a journal of concerns.* Use your scheduled worry time to write them down and brainstorm solutions. Often simply writing down your worry helps minimize it. Using this designated worry time effectively minimizes future worries.

3. *Stop telling yourself "stories."* Worriers spend a lot of time analyzing other people's actions and intentions. In the absence of facts, they tell themselves a whole story about the situation—usually with a negative outcome that causes further worries. I encourage Worriers to stop the stories and think only about the facts of a situation.

4. *Maintain a list of successful projects.* Worriers often operate from a fear of failure as opposed to expectation of success. This adds even more intensity to the way they approach projects. When the pressure is on I recommend taking a few seconds to review that list (keep it close by). Looking at your past track record of success has a calming effect and can help you move forward.

Practicing the above actions consistently free up so much "head time" for Worriers that they are able to move forward with more confidence and actually execute and produce results.

What developmental suggestions do you have for women who are Worriers and who overanalyze, freeze, or go quiet out of fear of failure?

Often, Worriers (and Pleasers) say 'yes' to every project that comes their way. They rarely say 'no.' Worriers are concerned that if they say 'no' it reflects on the perception of their ability to execute effectively in an organization. However, always saying 'yes' without the necessary resources will ultimately end in problems, as you will rarely have the bandwidth for adding multiple projects successfully long-term.

A better way to handle this for Worriers is to say, "Yes, but . . . I will need additional headcount/timeframe/budget to effectively execute this in addition to my current projects. Or we could review my current priorities and reallocate them in order to fit this in." Not saying 'no,' but highlighting how busy you currently are.

Consistently practice 1 – 4 above, and women will learn to manage their Worrier tendencies effectively.

Please share one of your best success stories in helping a women leader to advance in her career.

When I first met this executive, she had already been elevated to the executive leadership team and then swiftly demoted as she froze frequently in front of the board when making presentations. Although she was a brilliant woman, she did not invest time in building relationships and relied on a "command and control" way of directing subordinates and battling peers in order to achieve results. None of those behaviors work for sustained career success.

We worked together on the 1-4 techniques listed above. We also worked together on developing her communication skills—both presentations and focusing on listening and responding actively, plus relationship-building skills across the organization.

Today she is the president of a Fortune 1000 company, works directly and cohesively with a supportive board, enjoys positive relationships with her team, and, more importantly, has learned to be very effective and enjoy her success at work.

How important is it for aspiring women to gain a clear understanding of their inherent strengths, risks, and intrinsic motivators for success?

It's essential for women to have perspective on what drives their performance, what gives them joy, and what holds them back from fulfilling their potential. I'm certified in five different executive assessments. However, CDR Assessment is the one tool I use consistently because it provides executives with important insights into their behaviors. I know I will achieve swift and powerful change using this assessment tool with my clients.

What other advice do you have for aspiring women leaders?

Success is not defined for female leaders by role modeling your behavior after other male leaders. It's so important to be yourself. Know your strengths, own them, and use them on a daily basis. Naturally, a track record of successful results is important to progress in an organization. Don't expect everyone to automatically notice your success—it's important to do some self-promotion and strategically share your achievements with decision makers in the organization. Even more important is the ability to build positive relationships with your subordinates, peers, and bosses. Building success and maintaining multiple relationship bridges across a company ensures your ascent in the organization.

PATRICIA WHEELER, PhD

Managing Partner, The Levin Group LLC; Executive Coach
Atlanta, Georgia
Email: Patricia@TheLevinGroup.com

How have you helped women to overcome their Worrier risk behaviors?

With one senior vice president who tended to worry too much, we identified her inner dialogue during Worry mode. She reflected that during difficult conversations, she wondered, "How am I doing?" and "Am I messing up?" This hyper-internal focus prevented her from actively tackling the real issues facing her. She learned to anticipate these situations, take a brief break, and enter difficult conversations in a more relaxed and balanced manner. We identified more proactive areas of focus such as, "What is my message here?" and "What's important about this conversation?", which kept her more in the moment and less likely to worry.

What developmental suggestions do you have for women who are Worriers and who overanalyze, freeze, or go quiet out of fear of failure?

First of all, it's crucial to identify the following:

- When you go into this behavior, what are the thoughts, feelings, and sensations that alert you that you have entered the Worrier Zone?
- What are the most important triggers that tend to make you worry? For example, it may be the fear of confronting conflict, the concern that you are overstepping your bounds, or that you are making a mistake (that you imagine will haunt you).
- Conduct a regular review and "pulse check" on yourself several times a day. Ask yourself, "On a scale of 1 to 10, how worried am I?" Also notice what calms you down.
- Understand that when you enter the Worrier Zone, the cascade of Worrier neurochemicals takes around twenty minutes to exit your body. Take a break, take a walk, breathe deeply, and don't expect to have a brilliant turnaround moment at this time. You can turn things around later but never while you're still in Worry mode.
- When you are calm enough, evaluate the situation and plan your next steps to addressing the issue.

Ways to Practice Taming Your Worrier:

Be proactive. Review at the beginning of every day: "What may be most worrisome today? What outcome am I seeking? What are my best steps to achieving that outcome?"

Review at the end of the day: "What am I most proud of? To what degree did I get caught up in worrying? If so, how do I propose dealing with this next time? If not, what did I do to stay balanced and proactive?"

Maintain equilibrium. Regularly practice deep breathing. Stay hydrated and regularly stretch your muscles. Ensure that your life is balanced so that you don't overly attend to work issues.

Keep practicing. We all have default settings, and they don't go away completely. When you find good practices that help you stay balanced and focus on the important situations at hand, keep practicing these strategies even when you don't need to. Even elite athletes practice basic skills before and between important performances.

What's the best course of action for a woman who possesses the "Worrier" derailer?

Here are some steps that have helped my Worrier clients (excerpted from my 2015 Article, "Worry Less; Lead More"):

1. Take a good look in the mirror. If you have this characteristic, so be it. Understand that your worry is likely to be in excess of what many situations call for. If you realize you're likely to overreact under pressure, you can plan a more adaptive response in advance. One of my clients does advance planning every time she has a meeting scheduled with her very critical boss. She asks herself what he's likely to react to negatively, and mentally rehearses her messages to him. Doing so has diminished his perception that she's passive and reactive. Does this mean we can and should be able to eliminate worry? Of course not. Worrisome things do happen, but knowing that you are likely to overworry can help you anticipate situations where your Worrier may be triggered and plan appropriate coping strategies. Remember that this tendency need not define you and your leadership.

2. Manage your arousal. When we are under strong pressure, our biology changes; we move into a "fight or flight" mode. This causes us to create more adrenaline and cortisol. Think of these as the "unhappy neurochemicals" that help us escape actual danger (our biology hasn't really changed since we had to outrun saber-toothed tigers) but don't help us react adaptively to most workplace stresses. Recognize when you're under pressure, take a step back, and intentionally breathe more deeply and slowly. This small step actually helps our bodies regulate themselves out of the excessive worry zone. Find ways of reminding

yourself of your competence and plan in advance how you might better address recurring pressures without withdrawing into worry.

3. Embrace the positive. Scientists are finding increasing evidence that when we make the effort to acknowledge, embrace, and resonate with the positive events and emotions in our life, we increase our likelihood of success. We make better decisions, and we become better leaders. And we diminish the likelihood of being held captive by our derailers and default settings. The even better news is that we don't need to experience intense positive emotions to reap these benefits . . . what serves us best is to create and keep the habit of acknowledging what we appreciate and what's going well in our world.

These small changes in self-awareness and behavior can help us stay out of Worrier and stay in our most effective leadership behaviors. This, in turn, should help many talented women advance more effectively up the leadership pipeline.

ROSA ALGARRADA

Directora de Proyectos; Executive Advisor
Madrid, Spain
Email: rosa.algarrada@lyskam.com

How have you helped women to overcome their "Worrier" risk behaviors?

First, I listen to them and give them a space where they can express themselves. Then, I encourage them to place themselves in situations where they can feel talented and confident. Additionally, I use the CDR Assessment because it is a very comprehensive tool that helps women discover their areas of comfort and helps them make better decisions. As women become more aware of their risks through their CDR Assessment results, I help them find ways to leverage their strengths to minimize their risks. I help women realize that they have enough resources to grow and be successful. Furthermore,

I teach them to build trust with the people around them. This will help them worry, analyze, and stress less.

What developmental suggestions do you have for women who are Worriers and who overanalyze, freeze, or go quiet out of fear of failure?

It is important for women to have confidence in themselves and know that they have the resources they need to be successful. When they don't have enough confidence in themselves, it makes them more concerned about the impact their decisions have on others.

I often recommend they write a letter of appreciation to themselves. This letter should describe times when they have been there for themselves, haven't been demoralized, and have successfully overcome the challenges they faced. When they write themselves a letter of appreciation and recognition, they realize how capable and strong they have been in the past. It is a way for them to realize that they shouldn't be afraid to show the world who they are and what they are capable of. This letter is a very emotional experience that shows women all the times that they *could*. Sometimes, Worriers are afraid of themselves, and the CDR Assessment shows them that they have a vast amount of resources to support themselves.

Please share one of your best success stories in helping a woman leader to advance in her career?

I once worked with a woman who had reached her developmental peek in her role at her organization. She was looking for something more, but her worrier tendencies were holding her back. She was the type of person who was always worried about everything and everyone. She always wanted to make decisions that would benefit everyone else, and that was holding her back. As part of her coaching, she took the CDR Assessment. After reviewing her results and realizing her potential, she decided to leave her organization and start her own business. She took the leap of faith to become her own boss and work on something that benefits her community. She trusted her judgment and her ability to make bigger decisions on her own. Now that she believes in herself more, she worries less and acts more.

How important is it for aspiring women to gain a clear understanding of their inherent strengths, risks, and intrinsic motivators for success?

> It makes them more powerful. They look at themselves differently and crave to become a better person in all aspects of their life. They seek to develop themselves more.

What other advice do you have for aspiring women leaders?

> Women must have enough will to make things a reality. They should not give up after the first obstacle they encounter. Women should fight, look for people who add value to their lives, seek things they can lean and rely on.
>
> When it comes to making tough decisions, there are times when a women leader may want to discuss the issue with a trusted confidant or mentor to expedite her decision. These trusted individuals can listen and be a helpful sounding board and brainstorming partner. If a woman Worrier is stuck, sharing concerns or problems that are causing her to stall is better than dealing with the matter alone. Women need to be willing to stand strong and move forward and not freeze. They must have in mind that leadership is about helping and empowering others. People are not drawn to strategy initiatives; they are drawn to other people. If they are trustworthy, people will lean of them because they know the results will be well received by others.

LYNN HARRISON, PhD, MCC

Executive Coach, Black Tusk Leadership, Inc.
Whistler, British Columbia, Canada
Email: lharrison@blacktuskleadership.com

How have you helped women to overcome their "Worrier" risk behaviors?

> I have found that the first step in addressing "worrier" tendencies has been to recognize them and acknowledge their value. Usually a pattern develops because we have benefited from the behaviors in some way—for example, by considering

everything that might go wrong, or thinking through all the details, a woman leader may have produced high quality, impeccable results. However, when we overuse this approach, or engage in the pattern unconsciously, it can compromise the other strengths of our leadership style. In some cases, the worrier style may lead the person to be too cautious or hesitant to make decisions in situations where not all the information is available. Or, a fear of making a mistake can keep the leader from moving forward. As a result, she can be perceived as indecisive or lacking in confidence, eroding her personal power and leading others to question her ability to manage complex, difficult situations that call for courage and action.

Coaching that addresses the underlying causes and reasons for the worrier behavior can help dislodge this tendency. With greater awareness of the pattern, how it arises, and its impact, the person can begin to make other choices. Rather than reacting unconsciously, the woman leader chooses to be bold, to let go of having to have all the data, and to "swing for the fence". With some practice and support, (despite the experience of messiness this may initially involve), being able to perform without the weight of worry becomes a natural new pattern.

What developmental suggestions do you have for women who are Worriers and who overanalyze, freeze, or go quiet out of fear of failure?

I think that normalizing the pattern is helpful, as women leaders who are worriers are not alone in this behavior. Then, the leader needs to decide if she is up for trying something different and believe that change is possible. Is she ready to see herself as someone who is more than an expert or achiever? What kind of leader does she want to be?

If the leader is up for change, then it is important for her to start to notice what triggers her worrier response. There is usually some kind of perceived threat (fear of failure, discomfort with conflict, lack of confidence with a task or situation). Rather than protecting oneself with old responses like overanalyzing, turtling, or backing down, she takes the risk of acting differently. At first, this may be just a small step, like noticing her desire to run for the hills, to shut down, or to revisit the data. Just recognizing the moment is a great beginning. In trying out new responses (which may feel daring at first), it can helpful to ask for support from key stakeholders who have an interest in the leader's development. These caring people can provide the leader with specific feedback about what they observed and what else might work.

Please share one of your best success stories in helping a woman leader to advance in her career?

A leader I was coaching who was very competent at accounting was promoted to the CEO role in her company. This career advancement caught her by surprise, as she had not thought of herself as a CEO. She hesitantly decided to give it a go.

Smart, detail-oriented, hard-working, and responsible, this leader could be counted on to deliver the kind of results that her board was expecting. However, her attention to detail, tendency to micro-manage, and emotional distance did not facilitate trusting relationships among her executive team. The leaders experienced her "worrier" behaviors as questioning their capabilities. Each sought to prove to her that they knew their stuff. They found her too slow to make decisions and uninspiring because of her careful, cautious approach to things. The team wanted to see more passion from her, and the sense that she was as excited as they were about the future of the organization.

The leader did not realize that she was having this kind of impact until she received anonymous feedback from her team. She was shocked to learn that what she thought was conscientious, caring leadership was not being perceived as effective. She was taken aback by the gap in her self-ratings and those of her team.

To her credit, rather than make excuses or blame the group, this leader set about trying to change her pattern. She shared her feelings about the feedback and asked for the team's support in helping her to change. In our coaching sessions she was willing to explore the underpinnings of her cautious style. She resolved to express herself more directly in the here-and-now, rather than pondering on things inside or after meetings with her staff.

Step by step, she built confidence in herself and in her team. She showed that she truly had both backbone and heart—a willingness to make the tough calls and lean into the difficult conversations as well as to show that she cared about the team as individuals and as a group.

How important is it for aspiring women to gain a clear understanding of their inherent strengths, risks and intrinsic motivators for success?

I think that having good self-knowledge is critical for any leader. Without awareness of our strengths, we lack understanding of how to use our gifts and what serves our leadership well. If we do not know our risks, our Achilles' heel, we can be operating from blind spots that distract attention from our gifts. Our intrinsic motivators are what keep us going. Usually when we are doing work that does not fulfill our values or purpose, we cannot sustain the energy and enthusiasm that is needed, especially from a leader.

What other advice do you have for aspiring women leaders?

Bring all of yourself to your leadership. We don't need more women who are trying to be like men in the workplace. I know it is often not easy to get in the door, to be accepted in ranks occupied by mostly by men, or even to have a voice, but trust that we need you. Remember your essence and bring that to whatever you take on. Surround yourself with people who care about you, who believe in you, and who will remind you just how much you have to offer.

ELEVEN

Women: Tactics and Insights for Women to Develop Leadership Capability

"Success is an exception, so be exceptional."

—Malti Bhojwani

First: Self Awareness

Begin where it matters most and take steps to be *keenly self-aware.* We find—and the research strongly supports—that leaders tend to lack the clarity and personal objectivity needed to recognize, build upon, or leverage their inherent character talent, gifts, and acumen; while understanding, managing, and neutralizing their risks and short sides. This means that leaders spend a lot of time trying to develop the wrong things or having difficulty honing in on what matters most.

Next, women should ask and honestly answer the tough questions about themselves:

- Do I want to lead? Or do I want to be in a professional, team-oriented, or individual contributor role?
- What are my *true or inherent strengths*?
  - Am I a natural leader—do I naturally take charge whether I'm asked to or not?
  - How comfortable am I with making decisions?
  - Do I enjoy process rather than strategy?
  - Am I good at building relationships?
  - Am I sales oriented?
  - Do I have exceptional planning skills?
  - How assertive am I?
  - Am I skilled at negotiating?
  - Does delegating make me uncomfortable.
  - Do I enjoy presenting or is that one of my greatest fears?

The questions above are just to start you thinking. The best place to begin to think about formulating your career and leadership development action plan is by taking a deep dive approach. Gaining a clear sense of self, to a nuanced level, is the most important step you can take.

Know and Build Your Strengths

For example, consider the list of the seven personality character traits, provided earlier, which are an overview of one's strengths measured by the CDR Character Assessment with scoring ranges to consider.

TABLE 4
7 Character Traits

SCALE TITLE	HIGH SCORERS TEND TO BE DESCRIBED AS:	LOW SCORERS TEND TO BE DESCRIBED AS:
Adjustment	Calm, self-assured, easy-going, confident, steady under pressure, and may not be sufficiently self-critical	Self-critical, edgy, an intense performer, may push self and others and may not be as resilient to stress
Leadership Energy	Inclined to take charge, be leader-like and decisive, be interested in upward career mobility, and be highly competitive	Avoids leadership roles, prefers not to direct others or interact with those who are concerned with upward mobility as a measure for success
Sociability	Outgoing, extroverted, stimulated by talking with others, enjoys social interaction	Introverted tendencies, prefers less social interaction, maintains a lower profile, keeps to oneself, is quiet and perhaps shy
Interpersonal Sensitivity	Warm, caring, supportive, nurturing, sensitive toward the needs of others, interpersonally skilled, and perceptive	Task focused, hard-nosed, takes an objective approach, and is apathetic toward the needs of others

Table 4 continues on the next page.

TABLE 4 (CONTINUED)
7 Character Traits

SCALE TITLE	HIGH SCORERS TEND TO BE DESCRIBED AS:	LOW SCORERS TEND TO BE DESCRIBED AS:
Interpersonal Sensitivity	Warm, caring, supportive, nurturing, sensitive toward the needs of others, interpersonally skilled, and perceptive	Task focused, hard-nosed, takes an objective approach, and is apathetic toward the needs of others
Prudence	Practical, conscientious, self-controlled and disciplined, steady, reliable, stable, organized, and logical in a steadfast way	Spontaneous, risk taking, adventurous, potentially creative, adaptable and inventive
Inquisitive	Adventurous, clever, original, creative, imaginative, strategically focused and curious	Spontaneous, risk taking, adventurous, potentially creative, adaptable and inventive
Learning Approach	Typically seeks learning for the sake of personal enrichment, learns from wide range of media, and has academic interests	More interested in practical learning such as on-the-job training and hands-on or experiential learning

SOURCE: Nancy Parsons and Kimberly Leveridge, PhD, CDR Assessment Group, Inc., 1998.

The above traits on the CDR Character Assessment have strengths associated with both the high and low scores, but "desirable" scoring ranges depend on the job and competencies required.

With this assessment tool, the deep dive takes you to the subscales measured. This is where we learn about one's individual distinctions to pinpoint one's gifts and strengths or gaps to a very detailed level. Below is a sample of the subscales under Leadership Energy, with the high and low definitions.

ILLUSTRATION 3
Leadership Energy Subscales

Leadership Energy
Subscale Scoring Range Descriptions

Subscale Title	High Scores (50% and above) indicate:	Low Scores (49% and below) indicate:
Competitive	Persistent, competitive, driven, and enjoys the thrill of the chase	Not particularly competitive – prefers other methods to achieve rather than going against or trying to out do another
Self-Confident	Appears self-confident in a leadership capacity and determined	Lacks confidence or self doubting in leadership capability
Expects Success	See success as a reasonable expectation for virtually any task; positive outlook	Driven more by fear of failure rather than anticipating success; tends to be a realist; looks out for what can go wrong
Takes Charge	Enjoys leadership, takes initiative in groups and teams, is decisive	Less inclined to make decisions or assume authority over others
Career Focus	Strong sense of vocational identity, career path, and vision of future	Has career ambivalence; despite individual strengths, never quite sure about best career path
Presentation Confidence	Comfortable speaking to groups, strong platform presence	Anxious speaking in front of groups, may over-prepare or feel quite tense when required to present which can vary depending on who is in the group and the size of the group

SOURCE: Nancy Parsons and Kimberly Leveridge, PhD, CDR Assessment Group, Inc., 1998.

So, not to get into the weeds too far, but having a strength in Leadership Energy can manifest in a variety of ways, due to how one scores on the subscales. For example, if the leader candidate scores 65% overall on Leadership Energy, that might be broken down as follows:

Competitive 22%

Self Confidence: 100%

Expects Success: 11%

Takes Charge: 100%

Career Focus: 100%

Presentation Confidence: 59%*

*Percentages intentionally add up to more than 100%.

This translates to someone who

- is not prone to competing with others or staff (so likely not a candidate for a sales/marketing role);
- is confident in one's decisions and does not second guess them;
- expects things will get in the way of goals and anticipates potential problems in advance to establish contingency plans (this is common with engineers);
- is decisive, comfortable making decisions;
- is strategic and at ease with career direction; and
- has confidence in presenting but may experience some anxiety depending on certain groups one is presenting to.

Clearly, that is a lot of individual detail that is meaningful for developing one's potential as a leader and also determining the right type of leader roles to seek out.

When thinking about your personality traits or the preceding CDR Character scales, there are no good or bad scores. Ideally, you want to match your traits or scores with your key job duties. If these are in alignment, you will be working toward your strengths. High and low scores can be a strength, but the preferred range varies based on the job. For example,

- A *cold-calling* salesperson would need high Sociability and low Interpersonal Sensitivity to be most successful. In this way, they would be good at initiating discussions and meeting and greeting people, yet could deal with rejection easily and would not have a need to stay attentive to the client after the sale.

- A *relationship-building* salesperson would need high Sociability with mid- to mid-high Interpersonal Sensitivity. This salesperson, or account manager, would be good at taking care of customer needs and concerns for the longer haul.

- *Accountants* typically have mid- to high Prudence while software designers have lower Prudence with high Inquisitive scores.

Another way to think about gaining deep self-awareness—a critical element to developing most effectively as a leader or professional—is that it's like a spa experience for your career. Here is an excerpt from a blog article I wrote about re-energizing your career with a new level of self-awareness:

Do you want to re-energize, refocus, and make sure you are at your best? When is the last time you took time out to renew, refresh, and tend to your own well-being? Leadership and business demands can be exciting and can also be taxing, stressful, and sometimes exhausting. That is why you need to be at your best. Most of us commonly commit to resolutions about our physical fitness. However, we rarely, if ever, think in any serious way about getting our psyche and intrinsic motivators aligned with our career and life journey. I cannot tell you how many leaders say to me, after the initial coaching debrief with their CDR 3-D Suite of assessments, "I wish I had done this 20 years ago." One executive in pharmaceutical R&D wrote:

> "I cannot say enough good things about Nancy and her team at CDR. I just started my new job as a COO of a drug development startup when I saw Nancy speak at a conference. In her short 40-minute session at the conference, I knew immediately I could benefit from her help. Her approach to leadership coaching was immensely helpful. I gained valuable insights into my leadership style and I particularly enjoyed her session on how stress impacts me as a leader. That part of our session is something I use almost every day.
>
> As a scientist, the data-based assessment was very appealing and gave me some good data to relay on when discussing my role at the company with the board and my CEO. In addition, while the assessments were very thorough, what I enjoyed most was my one-on-one coaching session with Nancy. Her advice, opinion and experiential knowledge gave me some good perspective on my current job and also my future career. So much so that I wish I had done this years ago!" Elaine Hamm, PhD
>
> *(Since this letter in late 2017, she has become a CEO!)*
>
> SOURCE: Elaine Hamm, email to author, December 18, 2017.

Why wait any longer? Have you ever had coaching feedback that provided a clear and deep review of you leading to a new level of self-awareness? It is like a riveting spa for one's mind, career focus, and personal fulfillment.

There are a lot of jobs out there that are fascinating, complex, challenging, and rewarding. I am one of the lucky ones who can say mine is all of that and more. One of my primary responsibilities is coaching executives. I also train executive coaches how to use our assessments. On a rare occasion, I will assess and coach, as a favor to a colleague or family member, a college student to help them sort out what major and career might be best for them. I break it down to two simple things: 1) find what you are really good at; and 2) find what you love.

So, that is generally what our (CDR) executive coaches do—we help leaders and professionals find their true talent and their personal calling to joyful and rewarding work. However, we add another crucial factor to the mix to assure that this job fit and joyride blend does not fall off of its intended tracks. In our coaching debrief, we also pinpoint one's vulnerabilities or inherent risk factors that can undermine, or even derail, their success.

I'll take it down one notch further for clarity. Years ago, I presented at a Career Day for second graders. What we do, I explained, is help people understand their sunshine, stormy days, and what is in their hearts. (Of course, I used pictures and gave out heart-shaped *Charms* suckers to assure success.) Once people clarify or rediscover these things about themselves, I explained with more pictures, they can then drive their personal careers to the best, most prosperous, and happy places.

Getting back to my real job . . . My rewards are the "aha" moments, the shifts in thinking, and the radiant energy (glow) people have as they leave a coaching debriefing session. Rediscovering their strengths, facing and preparing to conquer their risks, and embracing what makes them happy is powerful and life changing. It is nearly impossible to accurately identify these traits, facets, and key themes without a skilled coach and well-constructed assessments. Further, people work so hard or have such busy schedules that there is typically no time left for their own career soul searching, fine tuning, and focus.

Our 2.5 hour coaching debrief session is that time out for a person to take a deep dive into exploring what makes them tick and what matters most. It is refreshing, invigorating, and highly productive for them from a development and performance standpoint. For me, no matter how tired or busy I may be, conducting a coaching feedback session is the best way to put a skip back in my step.

Don't let another year pass—take time out for your deep dive coaching session.

Clearly, the best way to get this new deep level of self-awareness is by taking a serious assessment tool like the CDR 3-D Suite *(and there are just a couple of others in this genre)* and having a qualified executive coach provide you with a comprehensive debrief. There are only a couple of these types of assessments on the market using a detailed Big Five personality measure, a risk or derailer assessment, and an intrinsic motivational measure.

What Are Your Risks and Vulnerabilities?

Then, consider your risks and vulnerabilities. Everyone has some level of risks because ineffective coping strategies under stress and adversity are part of normal personality.

Explore:

- What are my risk factors?
- How do I behave during conflict or with authority figures?
- Are my risks undermining my success and promotional visibility?

Chapter 12 provides details on how to develop your risks.

What Drives and Motivates You?

Drivers are strong. They "drive" behaviors and performance. In fact, when one's drivers are mismatched or are not respected by the manager and culture, this often results in lackluster performance and retention issues. So, while you may be a good job fit by way of experience and personality, if you are not happy or satisfied because your drivers are not being rewarded or endorsed, unhappiness and uninspired performance often set in. Further, if your drivers do not match the culturally dominant drivers, you may be more likely to feel as though you don't fit in. Ultimately, you may leave a company where your drivers are not in sync. Drivers are also known as your *deeply imbedded life interests* and they help you to find enjoyment and great satisfaction in your career and life.

The CDR Drivers & Rewards Assessment measures and describes the following:

- What really motivates you to excel

- Aspects of your work or career that provide you with a sense of enrichment and accomplishment

- The type of environment in which you will best perform (as well as describing those that would make you uneasy)

- The types (such as artists, executives, etc.) and quantities of people you enjoy working with

- How you want to be rewarded

- What level and kind of feedback and recognition is important to you

- The beliefs and philosophies you try to live by

- The types of activities that you should involve yourself in to stay satisfied with your work and life

It is important to identify and focus more clearly on your personal and career interests so that you can seek the roles, tasks, and projects that *match your personal drivers and motivators.* Pursuing a best fit in this arena is essential for at least six reasons:

1. Doing the type of work you enjoy is highly rewarding.

2. When you are content, happy, and relaxed you are likely to perform well.

3. This is powerful information to share with senior managers and team members to enlighten others about how you want to be treated, what types of tasks and roles you prefer and are likely to succeed in, and how you can best contribute to the team's and the organization's success.

4. On a team level, it makes sense for associates to share their Drivers & Rewards Assessment results with one another to match team roles with the most suitable team members as new projects and tasks arise.

5. It is not unusual for a person to find him or herself in a job that is less than satisfying. The Drivers & Rewards Assessment results provide information that is useful for career planning and development.

6. When your drivers and rewards needs are being met and satisfied, you cannot be simultaneously stressed, so this is an ideal way to manage your risk factors, including the Worrier trait. Think about it this way: when you are happy,

energized, and keenly interested in what you are doing, you cannot be negative or stressed out at the same time. That is why your drivers are so important. Not only do they help you perform better and feel happy with what you are doing, they also help you keep your risks from presenting. What a great way to prevent your risks from showing!

The following chart lists the 10 CDR Drivers & Rewards Assessment facets we measure. Which do you think you are drawn to and which do you find boring or non-interesting?

TABLE 5
Drivers and Rewards

DRIVERS AND REWARDS	DESCRIPTION
Business and Finance	Money, compensation or investments, economic issue
Artistic Endeavors	Creative expression or interests
Companionship and Affiliation	Close friendships in and outside of work
Fame and Feedback	Need for recognition, respect, praise, and visibility
Humanitarian Efforts	Desire for hands-on helping to directly assist the less fortunate
Amusement and Hedonism	Zest for life, strong sense of humor, likes to make work fun
Power and Competition	Status seeking, competitive, seeking upward mobility
Moral Platform	Life revolves around unwavering values and beliefs
Scientific Reasoning	Fascination with technology, scientific analysis and discovery
Safety and Security	Need for long-term financial, employment, and personal security

As you deepen your self-awareness, here are your next steps:

1. Ask yourself: Am I ready for this honest, deeper self-exploration process? What steps or actions do I need to take to get to my dream career goal or job? What might be slowing or stalling my success?

2. You may want to consider hiring a leadership or career coach, a skilled professional who uses validated assessments (including a risk assessment or derailment measure) to help you expedite this exploration process with accurate results. (We have many we can recommend!)

3. Most importantly: own your career. Your career mobility, planning, and success are your primary responsibilities.

Women who are Worriers and driven to lead, you especially must work on how to not let this risk make you seem or be judged to be "not leader-like." Do not allow this risk factor to take you out of the running! Don't wait for others to make you successful. Find where your strengths and capabilities lie, focus on what you love, and find the career that meets both of those areas for you. Remember, others can and will help you along the way, but you own the venture.

TWELVE

Analyzing and Developing Your Risk Factors

"The percentage of employees who believe they get no respect at work: 80%"

—The Cost of Bad Behavior
by Christine Pearson and Christine Porath

Identifying Your Risks

As noted throughout this book, personality-based risk factors are the culprits in undermining many careers, particularly those of women. So as part of the deep dive into self-awareness and development, it is crucial to identify, manage, and neutralize or prevent your risks from undermining your performance, communications, relationships, or promotability as a leader.

Ideally, it is best to take a validated risk assessment or use a de-railer type instrument. However, even without an instrument, you can carefully think about instances when you exhibited the following behaviors:

- Were less than as effective as you wanted to be
- Didn't speak up due to fear of not being 100% correct
- Allowed others to dominate airtime
- Were unable to articulate in an open and timely way
- Got mired down in work and probably go too far into the analysis or details
- Have set your own bar of expectations too high for yourself
- Held back knowing you were in disagreement, later to regret or drag your feet
- Dug into details way beyond what was necessary
- Were too slow in making a decision
- Shut down when conflict was high
- Failed to stand your ground due to others who were too aggressive
- Were too mistrustful and negative
- Asked far too many questions
- Used biting sarcasm that you had intended to be humorous
- Complained behind the scenes rather than deal openly with opposition or disagreements in the moment
- Said 'yes' when you wanted to say 'no'
- Held your tongue rather than take issue with your boss in front of others even though you knew he or she was wrong
- Expressed emotionality in an inappropriate way

The above examples represent *Moving Away* behaviors: Worrier, Detached, Hyper-Moody, Cynic, and False Advocate; and/or they represent *Moving Toward* behaviors: Pleaser and Perfectionist

Or, you can think about instances when you exhibited these following behaviors:

- Talked over others due to your passion
- Overstated your ability
- Said things that were taken as coming from left field or just weird
- Took too much of the credit
- Became condescending or demanding
- Lacked tact in communicating
- Had to have things your way and showed your stubbornness
- Went against convention and ignored policies you thought were not really relevant to you or your people
- Made impulsive decisions that were not the best
- Became too argumentative
- Tried too hard and pushed to the point of overselling
- Unintentionally became a bit disrespectful to others
- Talked too much
- Blurted things out without thinking that were not audience appropriate
- Dressed in ways contrary to social norms or business etiquette because you thought it was terrific

The above represents *Moving Against* behaviors: Egotist, Upstager, Rule Breaker, and Eccentric

The best way to get clear is to think about when things did not go as well as you had hoped. It is also extremely valuable to look at feedback from 360s, performance feedback, peer input, and any other developmental insights you have collected in the last couple of years. If your feedback providers have been open with you, this should give you nuggets of some of your risk behaviors. However, if input providers are either too kind or potentially fearful, this source of feedback may not hit the mark for you.

TABLE 6
Risks and Descriptions

RISK TRAIT	DESCRIPTION
False Advocate	Has passive-aggressive tendencies; appears outwardly supportive while covertly resisting
Worrier	Is unwilling to make decisions due to fear of failure or criticism
Cynic	Is skeptical, mistrustful, pessimistic, always looking for problems, constantly questioning decisions, resisting innovation
Rule Breaker	Ignores rules, tests the limits, does what feels good, risks company resources, does not think through consequences
Perfectionist	Micromanages, clings to details, has high need to control, has compulsive tendencies, sets unreasonably high standards
Egotist	Is self-centered, has a sense of entitlement and superiority, takes credit for others' accomplishments, is a hard-nosed competitor
Pleaser	Depends on others for feedback and approval, is eager to please the boss, avoids making decisions alone, won't challenge status quo, refuses to rock the boat
Hyper-Moody	Has unpredictable emotional swings, moodiness, volatility, potentially explosive outbursts, and vacillation of focus
Detached	Withdraws, fades away, fails to communicate, avoids confrontation, is aloof, tunes others out
Upstager	Excessively dramatic and histrionic, dominates meetings and airtime, is constantly selling a personal vision and viewpoint, demonstrates inability to go with the tide
Eccentric	Is quite unusual in thinking and behaving, perhaps whimsical, weird, out of social step or norms, peculiar in some ways

NANCY E. PARSONS

SOURCE FOR TABLE ON OPPOSITE PAGE: Nancy Parsons and Kimberly Leveridge, PhD, CDR Assessment Group, Inc., 1998.

Analyzing Risk Factors: A Step-by-Step Approach

This step-by step Risk Analysis Form is essential to help you manage and prevent your risks from undermining success. Of course, it is important for you to identify your specific array of risks with an appropriate assessment. If you have not taken an assessment tool, focus on the risk behaviors and identify the risk factor or two that you are fairly confident impacts you the most.

Once you have identified your risk factors you need to follow these steps to analyze your risks and to develop effective tactics and behaviors:

1. Think about when the risk behavior showed up the last few times. List several of these occurrences for each risk factor that you have.
2. What triggered the risk behaviors each time they showed up? (Who, circumstance, your state of mind, project, deadlines, uncertainty, conflict, what?)
3. How did the risk show up? Describe it fully. Please refer to the sample in the table below.
4. What was the impact or harm caused by the risk to you, your team, your leader, relationships, and/or to the business? In other words, what was the fallout and consequences?
5. Lastly, and most importantly—ask yourself what you can do differently in the future to prevent the risk behavior from undermining success or effectiveness. This is where you need to brainstorm ideas, tactics, and new approaches. Ideally, you should test your ideas with a mentor or coach or trusted advisor or colleague. Put these tactics into place. Anticipate and conquer the triggers with your new planned responses.

Additionally, you may want to consider times when you didn't go to your risk response and were successful. What was different about those situations that helped you move with your strengths? For example, maybe you hold back with a certain executive and one time you were unusually calm and direct. Why so? What helped you? Can you replicate this?

TABLE 7
Analyzing Risk Factors

The following table spans both pages.

MY RISK	WHAT CAUSED THIS RISK TO SHOW MOST RECENTLY?	HOW DID THIS RISK MANIFEST?
Upstager	Getting too energized during enjoyable discussion with colleagues.	Dominated too much of the air time.
Egotist	Overly eager to perform well and show my knowledge during presentation to Board.	Did not sufficiently recognize the contributions of other team members.
Rule Breaker	I was overly eager to close a deal with a client so I fudged the projected timeline.	Although I knew that the technical department needed 90 days to implement the new software for the client, I told them it could be done in 60 days or less.
Worrier	Fear of making sure I was 100% right. I was in a staff meeting.	As a director, at a meeting with my peers and boss I knew I had the right answer, but didn't speak up. I wasn't 100% confident that someone would not find a flaw.

TABLE 7 (CONTINUED)
Analyzing Risk Factors

MY RISK	WHAT WAS THE IMPACT?	WHAT CAN I DO DIFFERENTLY?
Upstager	Came off as negative, over-bearing, was a time hog.	Ask more questions, self-facilitate, deploy active listening skills, control my enthusiasm.
Egotist	Offended team; angered and hurt team members. Damaged team coopera-tiveness.	Try to relax more when I present. Build team mem-ber recognition into my presentation notes or slides so that I don't miss again! Apologize … Rebuild …
Rule Breaker	The technical director was furious and complained to my VP. The Tech team ended up working week-ends to finish and still missed my time promise by 10 days. The client wasn't happy.	Be more genuine in com-munications. I can still be enthusiastic without over-stating what we can do. Our technical team is top notch so I want to apolo-gize and let them know I will honor time require-ments in the future unless they approve changes in advance.
Worrier	The team made the wrong decision. Now we have to fix a costly mess which would have been avoided had I chimed in!	1) Find a mentor to help me practice speaking up in the moment. 2) Share my risks with a peer who will prompt me with ques-tions to help bring out my thoughts. 3) Register to take an assertiveness train-ing class.

SOURCE: Nancy Parsons and Kimberly Leveridge, PhD, CDR Assessment Group, Inc., 1999.

While you cannot train or wish away your inherent risk factors, you can make big strides to improve your risk reactions under adversity. You can adopt ways to prevent, neutralize, and manage these tendencies more productively. In baseball terminology, leaders can "improve their batting average" significantly when it comes to managing their risks.

Developmental Tactics and Ideas to Manage Your Risks

Once you know what your risk factors are and what (and who) triggers them for you, the next step is to brainstorm how to prevent or manage them more productively so that they do not interfere with performance or damage relationships. The following are some suggestions to help you improve your risk tendencies.

False Advocate:

- Avoid overcommitting rather than just taking on additional projects, clarifying deadlines and priorities can be helpful.
- Articulate concerns—don't go silent and hold back.
- Express ideas and thoughts *in the moment*—don't wait for a better time (in most cases).
- Ask clarifying questions to keep the discussion going; otherwise, going silent implies agreement.
- Ask for a timeout to think about things rather than just going silent in an implied agreement.

Worrier:

- Use a 70% rule—if you have thought about it a while and think it is about 70% ready, make the call or let it go!
- Ask a colleague (if you are overworking an issue) to help you cut to the chase.
- Set a time when you begin mulling things over—only allow 10 or 15 minutes. After that, move on!
- Don't be fearful—think of all of the past successes you have had and move forward!

Cynic:

- Check with a colleague to test your thinking and see if you are coming off too negative.
- Careful on the sarcasm—many may not think it is funny and it can be caustic or hurtful.
- Stop asking so many questions—give people a chance to get their ideas out before pouncing with 50 questions.
- Listen well and learn from optimists—maybe their positive approach will rub off a little!
- Find ways to show people that you TRUST them . . . be more open and supportive to them.

Rule Breaker:

- Identify boundaries as well as positive and negative consequences to your actions.
- Check your idea with another person who is not impulsive to get his/her take.
- Count to 10 and think—pause, before acting.
- Don't necessarily do it just because it feels good or seems fun; ask yourself: Why do I want to do this? and What can be the impact to others or yourself?

Perfectionist:

- Back off of the details—give people physical and psychological space.
- Check with coworkers about the amount of detail that is needed.
- Stop trying to control or get involved in everything.
- Ask your staff how much help on tasks or projects they want from you vs. acting from your own need for information or to have control.

Egotist:

- Show respect for others and learn how to value others more.
- Find out what the needs of others are and don't always put yourself first.

- Be kind, always.
- Pay attention to feedback and don't just dismiss it or disregard it.
- You are not perfect or the best at most things; read up on humility.
- Recognize others and give them credit for their work and accomplishments.

Pleaser:

- Ask clarifying questions; don't always just agree when you have a different opinion.
- Practice being more assertive in situations where you typically have a hard time speaking up—practice with someone safe!
- Learn how to set boundaries and learn to say no (or to articulate and negotiate priorities)
- Avoid working for an Egotist.
- Find a mentor or coach who can help you build more confidence and courage in speaking up; what you have to say matters.
- Don't suffer in silence—make your case!
- Assertiveness training may be something you should consider.
- Keep in mind, most managers WANT your feedback and suggestions.

Hyper-Moody:

- Step back; breathe deeply and slowly at least 3 times; take a time out.
- Don't' let your temper or mood get the better of you! Be kind and respectful!
- Ensure that your behavior is always consistent with your company's values.
- If you are really upset or shaken—take a break. Leave the room vs. saying something that you and others will find regrettable.
- Practice regular stress management techniques.

- Find the humor in things—it is hard to be stressed if you are laughing!
- You really need to manage your work/life balance.

Upstager:

- Time and pace yourself when speaking—refrain from dominating airtime!
- Stop pushing; don't oversell.
- Do not interrupt someone else who is speaking.
- Ask questions of others and give them plenty of time to speak.
- Have facilitated meetings so you and other Upstagers do not hog airtime—provide everyone a chance to speak and share ideas and thoughts.

Detached:

- Write down at least two questions you plan to ask at a meeting (and ask them!).
- Don't suffer in silence; when you feel pressured take a time-out and look at your watch to see how long you have been off by yourself. Go check in with someone. Possibly think about asking for help or assistance if a project has become too consuming.
- Let colleagues know about your tendency to detach and ask them to pull you back in when you have gone quiet for a while.
- Remember, hiding or withdrawing from a tough situation does not make it go away; try to push yourself forward to stay engaged.
- Perceptions and visibility are both important, so write down at least three ways you can become more visible at a meeting or within the company. Then, be sure to act on them and reward yourself when you do!

Eccentric:

- Run ideas by a trusted colleague before proposing them—especially on the important ones! This may help prevent you from blurting out things that may not be consistent with norms.
- If you tend to dress to your own artistic flare—consider finding a wardrobe specialist at a department store to help make sure you are in line with the appropriate, albeit creative, business attire for your work culture.
- Slow down when explaining how you arrived at certain ideas or positions; find ways to explain your thinking in a more logical way.
- Find a mentor or trusted colleague to review your performance at meeting; be sure they help you tag anything unusual.
- Ask for more feedback. Since you tend to march to your own beat, your perceptions and thoughts may be somewhat disconnected, so the more feedback, the better to stay tuned in.

Develop Your Executive Presence

"It is executive presence—and no man or woman attains a top job, lands an extraordinary deal, or develops a significant following without this heady combination of confidence, poise, and authenticity that convinces the rest of us we're in the presence of someone who's the real deal. It's an amalgam of qualities that telegraphs that you are in charge or deserve to be."
—*Sylvia Ann Hewlett*

Executive presence is a crucial element for success for the aspiring leader. Are you showing confidence and composure, and overall acting the part as we would expect an executive to do? The truth is that not all executives today have executive presence, but this is essential for a woman to develop and to gain essential visibility, particularly if she is a Worrier and holds herself back.

On the below table, the 7 Traits of Executive Presence[49] are summarized from Jun Medalla's article from *Business Insider*. Unfortunately, if a woman's Worrier trait is in high gear, most of these keys to executive presence can be thwarted. How the Worrier risk impacts each executive presence trait is described, along with tips to prevent this risk from undermining success.

TABLE 8
How Risks Can Impact the 7 Traits of Executive Presence

TRAIT OF EXECUTIVE PRESENCE	DESCRIPTION OF EXECUTIVE PRESENCE	HOW "WORRIER" RISK IMPACTS EACH EXECUTIVE PRESENCE TRAIT AND *TIPS TO PREVENT RISK FROM UNDERMINING YOUR SUCCESS*
Composure	The ability to control your emotions, recognize emotion in others, and manage your response to them.	Clearly, when a leader goes into the Worrier mode, they lose composure and freeze due to fear. This is when the effective responses are slow or do not happen. Emotion takes over, paralyzing effective action by the Worrier. *Work with a mentor, coach, or friend to practice or roleplay being relaxed despite uncomfortable challenges or when with people who may push your buttons. Anticipate the crowd or team in advance. Focus on your track record of success. Breathe, laugh, do things to make you relax in advance.*
Connection	It's critical to engage others when communicating and make them feel comfortable.	When a Worrier begins to overanalyze, freeze, and pull back, this inhibits the ability to engage effectively. If you do not feel comfortable, it is hard to help others feel that way. *Use your strengths (Interpersonal Sensitivity and Sociability) and charm to start each talk in a comfortable, informal way. Allow your strengths to take the lead. Practice this in safe networking situations.*

Table 8 continues on the following pages.

TABLE 8 (CONTINUED)
How Risks Can Impact the 7 Traits of Executive Presence

TRAIT OF EXECUTIVE PRESENCE	DESCRIPTION OF EXECUTIVE PRESENCE	HOW "WORRIER" RISK IMPACTS EACH EXECUTIVE PRESENCE TRAIT AND *TIPS TO PREVENT RISK FROM UNDERMINING YOUR SUCCESS*
Charisma	People who embody executive presence have the ability to draw others to them.	If a Worrier holds back or becomes too cautious, their natural charm and charisma can be hidden. Others pick up on trepidation, fear, and hesitancy. *Relax, breathe deeply 3 times (in and out), and be yourself! Shine!*
Confidence	One key aspect of executive presence is to communicate confidence both in what you say and how you say it. To appear confident, good posture and eye focus are critical. Ensure your facial expression matches your message and that your voice has good pitch, volume, and pace. And of course, you must look and dress the part.	The Worrier risk is the enemy of confidence. Allowing your Worrier risk to take over pushes your confidence out. Consider: do you look in people's eyes or avoid eye contact in fear? Do you shake hands solidly or like a wimpy washcloth? Do you dress professionally and in a way that enhances your confidence and messaging? *Take the time to evaluate your confidence and comfort level in key meetings, particularly with more senior level leaders. Are you relaxed? Do you feel equal to those in the room? Does your voice stay strong or crack or go too soft? Are you confident in your appearance? Of course, there are a myriad of actions to take if your Worrier risks inhibits your confidence. If it is your voice becoming shaky, work on it. If you have a concern about your appearance, hire an image or wardrobe consultant.*

TABLE 8 (CONTINUED)
How Risks Can Impact the 7 Traits of Executive Presence

TRAIT OF EXECUTIVE PRESENCE	DESCRIPTION OF EXECUTIVE PRESENCE	HOW "WORRIER" RISK IMPACTS EACH EXECUTIVE PRESENCE TRAIT AND *TIPS TO PREVENT RISK FROM UNDERMINING YOUR SUCCESS*
Credibility	Not only is your content important, but the language you choose to deliver it will impact your credibility. When someone with strong presence speaks, others take note, and there is no doubt of the conviction behind their words.	Obviously, the other executive presence traits above need to be conquered for your credibility to become clear. *What is ironic or sad with most Worriers is that they are often the most talented or most knowledgeable, yet they underplay this. Show and share what you know. When you don't, you not only hurt yourself and your visibility, you often hurt the team or the objective. This reminds me of show-and-tell as a child. Practice your show-and-tell—adult and leader version!*
Clarity	For you to exude presence, the ability to clearly communicate is fundamental. If your point is unclear, any hope of commanding attention is lost.	Clarity requires effective and timely communication. This means that the Worrier cannot hold back or freeze in fear. *You are the expert at what you do, so you need to practice clearly explaining your know-how or point of view. Practice with a peer, colleague, or mentor how to articulate clearly despite negative comments.*

Table 8 continues on the next page.

TABLE 8 (CONTINUED)
How Risks Can Impact the 7 Traits of Executive Presence

TRAIT OF EXECUTIVE PRESENCE	DESCRIPTION OF EXECUTIVE PRESENCE	HOW "WORRIER" RISK IMPACTS EACH EXECUTIVE PRESENCE TRAIT AND *TIPS TO PREVENT RISK FROM UNDERMINING YOUR SUCCESS*
Conciseness	Being verbose kills presence. Just as it is critical to know what you want to communicate, you must be able to do it concisely. Once you've delivered your message and validated it briefly, reverse back to others by asking, "What else can I share with you about this idea?" This way, you stay on point and only expand on a topic with the content that your listener needs.	Conciseness should not be a direct issue for the Worrier. However, other risks like Upstager and Perfectionist might cause the Worrier to dig into the details too much. *Practice your verbal explanation skills and tape them. Listen to these with your mentor or peer/friend to make sure you are being appropriately direct and concise. Get good at getting to the point. Practice more if helpful.*

SOURCE: Nancy Parsons and Kimberly Leveridge, PhD, CDR Assessment Group, Inc., 1999.

There are many books, training workshops, and executive coaches who specialize in helping leaders enhance their executive presence skills.

THIRTEEN

Cultural Study Shows Bias Is More Damaging Than Most Think

"When we listen and celebrate what is both common and different, we become a wiser, more inclusive, and better organization."

—Pat Wadors

A real cultural bias has developed and become ingrained in us since the early history of humankind. Normal human biases do not equate to intentional, malevolent discrimination. However, perceptions about gender in leadership are considerably worse for women than most people think. This is where training, education, group facilitation, and diversity workshops can help. While business people and academics alike understand this, the crux of the matter is that many leaders and professionals still accept and endorse gender misperceptions without consciously realizing they are doing so or realizing the extent of its damage.

Alison Quirk of State Street Corp., also at the forum attended by Jack Welch, stated: "We can all do more to help people understand their unconscious biases." [50] Ms. Quirk is right. The term "unconscious bias" can be off-putting because most of us think we are fair and objective—at least that is our intent. Howard Ross eloquently explains the impact of unconscious perceptions:

> Unconscious perceptions govern many of the most important decisions we make and have a profound effect on the lives of many people in many ways. . . . Unconscious patterns can play out in ways that are so subtle they are hard to spot. [51]

Perhaps "perceptions" is a more acceptable term, but regardless, everyone has some set of biases or lenses with which they view people, issues, and more. At CDR Assessment Group, Inc., we have studied this very point: biases *versus* personality characteristics. What we found is a real chasm between the performance tendencies or the personality traits of women versus the related perceptions of those behaviors. Misplaced perceptions, unconscious biases, and gender stereotypes tend to be more negative or punitive towards women while inaccurate perceptions often catapult men forward. Clearly, while women's Worrier risk factor frequently undermines success and upward trajectory, what is also compelling is that the harsh judgments or perceptions against women are more starkly damaging than most realize.

Rubbing Salt in the Wounds:
Biases Holding Women Back

Table 9 supports Ms. Quirk's contention that unconscious bias is holding women back far more than demonstrated performance or capability are. The table is from our presentation, titled "Risk Factors that Impact Women in Leadership," which we presented at sessions for the Association of Talent Development (ATD), the Executive Women's Forum (EWF), and the Women's Business Council Southwest (WBCS). Our data show the damaging yet different perceptions that often stem from the *same* leadership risk behavior. Table 9 lists the words others have used to label men and women with the same risks, which was based on a literary review of gender biased language. As you will see, the words used to label their perception of the women are far more negative, and therefore detrimental, than those of the men with the same risks.

TABLE 9

CDR Assessment Risk Factors and Unconscious Bias

CDR RISK ASSESSMENT SCALE DESCRIPTION	WOMEN LEADERS DEMONSTRATING THIS RISK PERCEIVED OR FREQUENTLY LABELED AS:	MEN LEADERS DEMONSTRATING THIS RISK PERCEIVED OR FREQUENTLY LABELED AS:
FALSE ADVOCATE Passive-aggressive tendencies; appears outwardly supportive while covertly resisting	Sneaky, spreads rumors	Quiet dissenter
WORRIER Unwilling to make decisions due to fear of failure or criticism; is indecisive, overanalyzes; is self-doubting	Afraid, fearful, indecisive, lacking courage	Thoughtful decision maker
CYNIC Skeptical, mistrustful, pessimistic, always looking for problems, constantly questions decisions, resists innovation	Nasty, pessimistic, paranoid	Investigative mind, sarcastic
RULE BREAKER Ignores rules, tests the limits, does what feels good, risks company resources, does not think through consequences	Inconsistent, untrustworthy	Change agent, maverick

Table 9 continues on the next page.

TABLE 9 (CONTINUED)
CDR Assessment Risk Factors and Unconscious Bias

CDR RISK ASSESSMENT SCALE DESCRIPTION	WOMEN LEADERS DEMONSTRATING THIS RISK PERCEIVED OR FREQUENTLY LABELED AS:	MEN LEADERS DEMONSTRATING THIS RISK PERCEIVED OR FREQUENTLY LABELED AS:
PERFECTIONIST Micromanages, clings to details, has a high need to control, has compulsive tendencies, sets unreasonably high standards	Micromanager, nitpicker	Good eye for detail
EGOTIST Self-centered, has sense of entitlement and superiority, takes credit for others' accomplishments, is a hard-nosed competitor	"Self-absorbed bitch" *"Dragon lady"*	Overconfident
PLEASER Depends on others for feedback and approval, is eager to please the boss, avoids making decisions alone, won't challenge status quo, refuses to rock the boat	Ingratiating, subservient	Good soldier, loyal
HYPER-MOODY Unpredictable emotional swings, moodiness, volatility, potentially explosive outbursts, and vacillation of focus	Too emotional or "it's that time"	Intense, passionate

Table 9 continues on the next page.

TABLE 9 (CONTINUED)
CDR Assessment Risk Factors and Unconscious Bias

CDR RISK ASSESSMENT SCALE DESCRIPTION	WOMEN LEADERS DEMONSTRATING THIS RISK PERCEIVED OR FREQUENTLY LABELED AS:	MEN LEADERS DEMONSTRATING THIS RISK PERCEIVED OR FREQUENTLY LABELED AS:
DETACHED Withdraws, fades away, fails to communicate, avoids confrontation, is aloof, tunes others out	Non-assertive, shy	Reserved, thoughtful
UPSTAGER Excessively dramatic and histrionic, dominates meetings and airtime, is constantly selling a personal vision and viewpoint, demonstrates inability to go with the tide	Too opinionated	Sells point of view
ECCENTRIC quite unusual in thinking and behaving, perhaps whimsical, weird, out of social step or norms, peculiar in some ways	Not well grounded, weird	Abstract thinker

SOURCE: Nancy Parsons and Kimberly Leveridge, PhD, CDR Assessment Group, Inc., 1998.

Comparing CDR Assessment Results to
the Pew Social Trends Survey Data

In Examples 1– 5 below, our data further show that people are not as harsh or punitive in their judgments toward men's behaviors as they are with women's, even when they share the same character risks. When comparing the Pew Social Trends Survey results to our CDR Character and Risk Assessments, the differences are stunning. It is clear that, as pointed out in the first part of Chapter 3, false perceptions and erroneous stereotypes hurt women leaders far more than they hurt male leaders. While comparing the Pew Survey to CDR Assessment results, we found five examples:

1. There are *no significant differences* between the "emotionality" of men and women despite perceptions suggesting that huge differences exist.

2. Women are not more manipulative then men, however, how they manipulate is different.

3. In healthy work environments, women are more outgoing, which agrees with perceptions. However, under conflict and stress, men tend to be more aggressive and may dominate airtime.

4. Women leaders *do* tend to be more compassionate and communicate with more charm and concern based on their Interpersonal Sensitivity scores combined with their Sociability. Women are better at relationship building.

5. Men tend to come across as more arrogant and overly confident, particularly when facing adversity.

Example 1

Pew survey respondents rate women as the more *emotional* sex than men by 85% to 5%.

What the CDR Assessment profile data results say:

CDR ASSESSMENT SOURCE	CDR SCALE TITLE	WOMEN LEADERS AVERAGE SCORE	MEN LEADERS AVERAGE SCORE
Character	Adjustment	50%	54%
Risk	Hyper-Moody	62%	56%

What does this mean?

There are *no significant differences* between the "emotionality" of men and women when stress is low, based on similar Adjustment scores. When facing adversity, women may be slightly more emotional, according to their Hyper-Moody risk factor.

How emotionality is judged or perceived is *frequently based on gender bias.* For women, emotionality is often *confused* with Interpersonal Sensitivity or nurturing/caring and relationship-building capability. These are different constructs. Emotionality has to do with temperament and changing moods; high Interpersonal Sensitivity is about showing care, nurturing, kindness, and helpfulness.

Emotionality of male leaders is often associated with anger, impatience, etc. and is considered an *accepted* behavior in most organizations. Additionally, men may be more likely to hide emotionality better than women.

Example 2

Pew survey respondents rate women as more *manipulative* than men by 52% to 2%.

What the CDR Assessment profile data results say:

CDR ASSESSMENT SOURCE	CDR SCALE TITLE	WOMEN LEADERS AVERAGED SCORE	MEN LEADERS AVERAGED SCORE
Risk	False Advocate	61%	55%
Character	Inquisitive	50%	59%
Risk	Rule Breaker	53%	64%

What does this mean?

False Advocate is higher for women leaders so there will be more inclination for them to complain behind the scenes—this can manifest as the martyr or victim syndrome. Male leaders may *manipulate* or "jockey for position" in bolder ways due to Rule Breaking and Inquisitive scores.

However, the drastic difference of *52% to 26% in the Pew survey is not supported by the CDR data a*nd is perhaps exaggerated by biased perceptions.

Example 3

Pew survey respondents rate women as more *outgoing* than men by 47% to 28%t.

What the CDR Assessment profile data results say:

CDR ASSESSMENT SOURCE	CDR SCALE TITLE	WOMEN LEADERS AVERAGED SCORE	MEN LEADERS AVERAGED SCORE
Character	Sociability	63%	57%
Risk	Upstager	60%	66%
Risk	Worrier	63%	48%

What does this mean?

In *healthy* work environments where character strengths manifest more, women leaders are more *outgoing*. Under pressure and conflict, men leaders tend to be pushy and dominate airtime based on their Upstager risk. Under pressure, many women leaders tend to move away and not speak up, influenced by their Worrier risks.

Example 4

Pew Survey respondents rate women as more compassionate than men by 80% to 5%.

What the CDR Assessment profile data results say:

CDR ASSESSMENT SOURCE	CDR SCALE TITLE	WOMEN LEADERS AVERAGED SCORE	MEN LEADERS AVERAGED SCORE
Character	Interpersonal Sensitivity	56%	40%
Character	Sociability	63%	57%
Risk	Egotist	53%	61%

What does this mean?

Women leaders *do* tend to be more compassionate and communicate with more charm and concern based on their Interpersonal Sensitivity scores combined with their Sociability.

Male leaders tend to be more direct due to their lower Interpersonal Sensitivity scores. Under stress, men may intimidate or be pushy, as indicated by their Egotist scores. Male leaders have a sufficient level of compassion, as they still fall within the mid-range on Interpersonal Sensitivity.

Example 5

Pew Survey respondents rate men as the more arrogant sex by 70%.

What the CDR Assessment profile data results say:

CDR ASSESSMENT SOURCE	CDR SCALE TITLE	WOMEN LEADERS AVERAGED SCORE	MEN LEADERS AVERAGED SCORE
Character	Adjustment	50%	54%
Risk	Egotist	52%	61%
Risk	Upstager	60%	66%

What does this mean?

Men tend to come across as more arrogant and overly confident, particularly when facing adversity, as can be seen with their Egotist and Upstager scores. Arrogance is thought of as part of the common makeup of leaders (or even as acceptable). Arrogance is a trait more commonly held by men, as shown in the CDR research and the Pew survey results.

The data comparisons from the examples demonstrate that the biases are either incorrect, skewed, or significantly exaggerated. For instance, Example 1 compares emotionality as exhibited by men and women. In the Pew Survey, 80% of respondents rated women as the more emotional sex, compared to 5% for men. Yet, the personality data shows "there are no significant differences between the 'emotionality' of men and women." This means that cultural perceptions are far harsher toward women and more forgiving of men. Men's bad behaviors are accepted or ignored. The same behaviors from women, on the other hand, can end any further upward career progress.

Why Is This Research So Compelling?

Our personality traits—both character and risks—are inherent, so we cannot change these in any significant way by wishing, hoping, or even training. Once we reach working-adult age, our personality traits have become our ingrained behaviors. These are set. We can certainly enhance skills to a certain degree. We can manage and neutralize our risk behaviors with self-awareness and by deploying effective tactics to prevent damaging behaviors. However, we cannot change our personality traits (strengths or risks) in a whole scale way.

For example, if someone is very extroverted, that person will not become an introvert, short of a mind-altering accident or injury. The same goes for a Worrier. If one has this trait, this will also tend to present, given the stimuli and conditions that bring it about for a person. Now, training and development can help one to manage their risks more productively or even to prevent the risks from occurring in certain cases, but the tendency to worry will still appear from time to time.

There is Good News: Perceptions of Women's Ability to Lead

According to the Pew Survey of Women and Leadership 2018, "Americans largely see men and women as equally capable when it comes to some of the key qualities and behaviors essential for leadership" Additionally, while most reported men and women have different styles, few think that one gender has a better overall approach.[52]

ILLUSTRATION 4

Pew Survey of Women in Leadership 2018

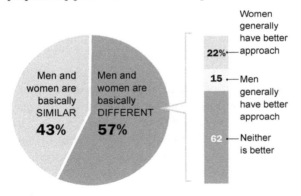

Among those who say men and women have different leadership styles, most say niether has a better approach

% saying that when it comes to the leadership styles of people in top positions in business and politics ...

Note: Share of respondents who didn't offer an answer not shown.
Source: Survey of U.S. adults conducted June 19-July 2, 2018.
"Women and Leadership 2018"

PEW RESEARCH CENTER

About 6 in 10 say there are too few women in leadership posts.[53]

ILLUSTRATION 5

How Americans Rate Ambition and Assertiveness of Those Seeking Executive Roles by Gender

---

Americans see assertiveness, ambition as more helpful to men than women seeking top executive positions

% saying each of the following _____ a man's/woman's chances of getting a top executive business position

		Mostly helps	Mostly hurts	Not much difference
Being assertive	A man's chances	73	5	20
	A woman's chances	53	24	24
Being decisive	A man's chances	74	4	21
	A woman's chances	63	10	26
Being ambitious	A man's chances	71	6	22
	A woman's chances	54	20	24
Being approachable	A man's chances	60	5	34
	A woman's chances	58	9	31
Being physically attractive	A man's chances	54	4	41
	A woman's chances	69	8	21
Being compassionate	A man's chances	29	22	47
	A woman's chances	35	27	37
Showing emotions	A man's chances	8	58	33
	A woman's chances	10	65	24

Note: Share of respondents who didn't offer an answer not shown.
Source: Survey of U.S. adults conducted June 19-July 2, 2018.
"Women and Leadership 2018"

PEW RESEARCH CENTER

There are two additional characteristics that the public sees as more helpful for men to reach leadership roles in politics and business than for women with similar aspirations: ambition and decisiveness. Roughly seven-in-ten adults say ambition is a helpful trait for a man to have, while almost half say ambition helps women get ahead. About one-in-five say that being ambitious mostly hurts women in both politics and business. When it comes to being decisive, roughly seven-in-ten adults say being decisive helps men to succeed in either politics or business, while six out of ten say this about women.[54]

According to Erica Jaffe in a *Fast Company* article,

> Behavioral evidence compiled over the past two decades suggests workplace gender bias not only persists but thrives in ways many of us don't even realize, particularly for women in

male-dominated professions. These stereotypes are so embedded in the cultural brain that we often serve them without being aware.[55]

Authors Caryl Rivers and Rosalind C. Barnett's book, *The New Soft War on Women: How the Myth of Female Ascendance Is Hurting Women, Men, and Our Economy*, compiles an abundance of research to show that "office sexism still exists, it's just less blatant than it used to be."[56]

> Despite evidence that men are typically perceived as more appropriate and effective than women in leadership positions, a recent debate has emerged in the popular press and academic literature over the potential existence of a female leadership advantage. This meta-analysis addresses this debate by quantitatively summarizing gender differences in perceptions of leadership effectiveness across 99 independent samples from 95 studies. Results show that when all leadership contexts are considered, men and women do not differ in perceived leadership effectiveness. Yet, when other-ratings only are examined, women are rated as significantly more effective than men. In contrast, when self-ratings only are examined, men rate themselves as significantly more effective than women rate themselves.[57]

Unfortunately, in today's processes, perceptions and biases are the key to making decisions when it comes to promotions, succession planning, development, and selection process. This makes it imperative that we add objectivity early on in the process, which is why scientifically validated personality and motivational instruments are pivotal. These instruments are gender/race-neutral and are essentially blind in terms of biased judgments. For example, when I receive a candidate's data to review for succession planning, the sole consideration factor is the candidate's score—race, gender, and sex are out of the question. The candidate's score includes results from self-report questionnaires, which are scored based on competencies key to success in given positions. Until we systemically add this type of objective tool, naturally biased perceptions will keep the doors shut for aspiring women.

FOURTEEN

Action Plans and Solutions for Glass Ceiling Stakeholders (Including the C-Suite)

"If your actions create a legacy that inspires others to dream more, learn more, do more and become more, then, you are an excellent leader."

—*Dolly Parton*

Who Are the Stakeholders?

Women have the power to take charge of their own careers, manage and neutralize their Worrier risk, and to rise to the highest levels of leadership. The more women take charge and fully utilize their power, the more rapidly the glass ceiling will begin to dissipate.

Next in line to support women's successful ascent are executives as key stakeholders. Leadership development experts and diversity and inclusion leaders are also stakeholders who can improve services that support women. The four stakeholder groups that can help drive and support the solutions forward are

- C-Suite Members/Executives
- Talent/Leader Development Experts
- Interest Groups
- Individuals

ILLUSTRATION 6
Who Are the Glass Ceiling Solution Stakeholders?

SOURCE: Nancy Parsons, CDR Assessment Group, Inc., 2016.

160

Though there may be some crossover among tasks, each group has a clear, distinct role in designing and implementing the solutions necessary to bring down the glass ceiling for good, therefore, it is imperative that stakeholders provide support and services.

The key to success, as with any performance initiative, is solid commitment and accountability. It is in the hands of senior leaders to take charge in leading a social change, and if the C-Suite members and board of directors fail to fulfill their role to champion change, systemic success may be stymied. Ending the glass ceiling is an achievable goal, but we must change traditional approaches.

The other enemy to executives' success is delegation. As mentioned previously, too many executives wash their hands of the glass ceiling issue when they pass the baton to a designated "diversity manager." This is not effective. Diversity managers are essential to disseminate the message, facilitate training, design new development approaches, and take a lead with the effort, but they should not be the lone leader on this mission.

Key Roles of Stakeholders

Illustration 7 provides an overview of what each stakeholder group should do to help bring down the glass ceiling.

ILLUSTRATION 7
Key Roles of Glass Ceiling Stakeholders

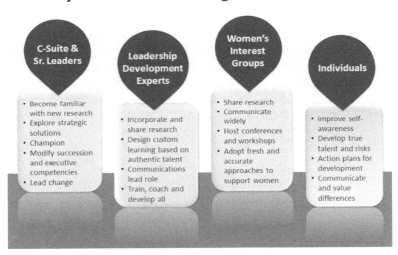

Key Roles of Glass Ceiling Solution Owners

C-Suite & Sr. Leaders
- Become familiar with new research
- Explore strategic solutions
- Champion
- Modify succession and executive competencies
- Lead change

Leadership Development Experts
- Incorporate and share research
- Design custom learning based on authentic talent
- Communications lead role
- Train, coach and develop all

Women's Interest Groups
- Share research
- Communicate widely
- Host conferences and workshops
- Adopt fresh and accurate approaches to support women

Individuals
- Improve self-awareness
- Develop true talent and risks
- Action plans for development
- Communicate and value differences

SOURCE: Nancy Parsons, CDR Assessment Group, Inc., 2017.

The starting point for all is to share this research. Study it. Analyze it. Debate it. Explore the implications in the organizations you serve or support. Find ways for each group to develop the solutions to this systemic problem, like those suggestions described below. Keep in mind that all groups need to begin moving in the right direction. It can't just be the women or the academics—we really need to begin a positive *movement* to end the glass ceiling.

C-Suite and Senior Leaders

Executives, boards, and senior leaders need to become familiar with the research and findings shared in this book. Sharing this objective data will help them see the business opportunities for what they are. It will help them realize that the solutions—based on the research results—are practical, objective, and crucial to ending the glass ceiling.

One of the best ways to do this is to have a skilled facilitator/consultant at a senior-level meeting with ample time scheduled to present the findings and to facilitate a dialogue with team members. Objectives for the senior leadership team are as follows:

- **Recognize that the glass ceiling is a real problem.** It hurts the bottom line and needs their direct support and leadership. They should explore the performance impact on their own bottom lines.
- **Realize that this is not in any way a "bash-the-men" or combative issue.** This is transformative for businesses because we are asking leaders at all levels to start looking more objectively and directly at what contributes to leadership success. To do this, we need to objectively identify leadership talent, develop both women and men based on their own true talent, and hold them accountable for their performance.
- **Model the way.** Senior leaders need to serve as champions to lead the changes. Come up with solutions that will work for their business or follow the process outlined below.

The C-Suite and senior leader orientation and discussion process should cover the following:

- The glass ceiling research findings: a review of the differences between men and women's inherent risks that manifest under pressure (men tend to *Move Against* and fight; women tend to be Worriers who *Move Away* and avoid tough situations or conflict.)
- Explore why perceptions are skewed—women are judged more harshly and negatively, often for the same behaviors exhibited by men. Consider the perceptions demonstrated in the organization.

- A review of the performance and financial consequences of allowing the above points to hold women back. Ideally, a model should be developed and the fiscal impact on the organization should be calculated and presented.

  1. As an example, the study of 21,980 global organizations from 91 countries conducted in 2016 by Peterson Institute for International Economics, which we covered previously, found that companies with at least 30% female leaders—in senior management positions—experienced a 15% increase in profitability.[58]
  How would an increase of about 15% in profitability impact the company?

  2. A study of 4,000 public companies from across the globe, published by MSCI Research in November 2015, found that "companies that had strong female leadership generated a Return on Equity of 10.1% per year versus 7.4% for those without."[59]
  How would a 2.7% increase in return on equity impact the organization?

  3. And last, we saw how female leaders were rated higher on 360° reviews in a study by Jack Zenger and Joseph Folkman of 7,280 leaders. It was reported that "at all levels, women are rated higher in fully twelve of the sixteen leader competencies measured."[60]
  How would this impact bottom line performance, employee retention, and customer loyalty? Can this be measured?

- Financial and performance indicators should be looked at and the numbers related to the positive benefits of having women in higher leadership positions should be run and presented.
- A review of existing Executive Competency Models and Succession Planning Criteria. No longer should *only* those who fight with aggression under adversity be viewed as promotable or "leader-like." Discuss and consider:

1. Are the company's competency models or succession planning evaluation methods naturally screening out more women than men? Why so? Is the gap significant?

2. Equipped with the findings in this book, could a change be implemented in the current promotability ratings or developmental opportunities for women who may have high potential but who would have otherwise been ignored?

3. Do more men appear promotable because they are assertive (or even aggressive) under tough or challenging situations?

4. Do fewer women than men seem to rise to the top of succession plans or be considered for promotion?

5. Should the Worrier trait be a valid reason not to consider female leadership candidates? Or is there another way to look at this or address this situation?

6. Is the company using a scientifically valid assessment instrument to measure inherent leadership strengths and talents as well as risk factors? Should it be? What might be missing? What does a cost/benefit analysis yield on this?

7. Other topics, concerns, and analysis relevant to the organization and industry.

Moving forward, the C-Suite and senior leaders would benefit from the following:

- **Be willing to dedicate** time and financial resources needed for the solution. Develop the customized authentic leadership training and individual coaching budget to help women (and men) develop their strengths while managing their differing risks. Communicate and promote this new awareness and appropriate cultural changes throughout your organization and at industry forums. Conduct employee meetings, develop short videos, and host web conferences to discuss. Begin leading the cultural shifts.

- **Gain appreciation** for the fact that leaders should be diverse in their inherent profiles (strengths and risks) and that this is a good thing. However, with the richness of diverse strengths and talents comes the need for personalized leadership development. Cookie-cutter, male-dominated leadership evaluation models and training designs are no longer viable.

- **Stop rewarding** *Moving Against* behaviors as the only ticket to success in the organization.

- **Review and use the "Summary of Eight Practical Steps to End the Glass Ceiling"** in Chapter 15 in order to begin focusing on clear action plans for your team and for others to perform throughout the organization. These give you some practical steps to take.

- **Hold yourself, your team, leaders, and others throughout the organization** *accountable*. Establish and enforce leadership expectations and accountability. While all humans and leaders have some level of risk factor traits, it does not excuse poor behavior.

Fix the System: Making Gender-Neutral, Objective Succession Planning and Promotional Decisions

As noted above, it is important to revamp succession planning systems in order to identify, develop, and promote more women. Succession planning is a systemic approach for an organization to identify and develop key leadership and professional talent to ensure sustainment for future performance success. This provides the formula to identify and develop talent from within to enhance retention, loyalty, customer relationships, competitive position, knowledge, and stockholder confidence. The problem is that the current approach is not working and, by design, frequently excludes or hinders high-potential women while including more men who, in many cases, are not as capable.

How can we improve this flawed system? We need to add science to the process. Women will continue to be held back prematurely until well-constructed, scientifically valid assessments measuring personality character traits, risks for derailment, and motivational facets are used at the front end of the process. Today's succession planning system generally relies on the same inputs they always have:

- Performance reviews
- 360° feedback
- Recommendations
- Job/educational history
- Salary and bonus records

The above is not enough. Unfortunately, most of this list is based on subjective judgments and are, therefore, naturally biased towards one's own perspectives and tastes, and they provide only small snapshots—at best—of a person's capabilities. Key talents, gifts, and capabilities are often over- or undersold, or just missed in the consideration. Succession planning today depends to a great extent on how well a sponsor can sell a candidate or win the debate—another non-objective technique.

Another significant issue is that with succession planning, very little, if any, attention is paid to a candidate's personality risk factors, and these are of paramount importance to future success. When risk factors are ignored and, worse yet, some are essentially rewarded by a promotion or labeled as a sign of an up-and-comer, this feeds the ego and allows the risks to continue without recognition or accountability.

That is, unless you are a woman. As a woman, your risks (particular as Worriers) dismiss you from the *high potential* discussions before they begin. You're overlooked and no longer appear to be a courageous or leader-like figure. You are viewed as a real doer. You execute, implement, and serve as the backbone to the team's productivity, but not seen as a leader. Also, because Worriers frequently undersell themselves, so do their bosses. Worriers often make their bosses look good, so you might be a real keeper.

Accurate, scientifically validated personality (strengths and risks) and motivational assessments should be included as an early step of succession planning for identifying and developing high potential leaders. With assessments at the front end there should be two goals:

1. Objectively identify the organization's current bench strength.
2. Identify each individual's best strengths, acumen, vocational capability, interpersonal skills, leader voice, competency fitness, risk factors (potential derailers), vulnerabilities, and incentive and reward needs.

The individual capability assessments provide the management team with the framework for the candidate's best talents and suitability for specific promotional opportunities and upcoming key executive job vacancies. Additionally, the results provide a clear road map for developmental actions that reflect the needs of the individual in harmony with the key position requirements for which the candidate is expected to succeed.

Once the assessments are administered to the respective talent pool, the experts use the aggregate results to reveal the current bench strength of the organization. This analysis will show any gaps, lopsidedness, and distinct strengths. A competitive benchmark analysis is also typically performed. These findings, used in conjunction with the client's strategic business objectives, provide a framework to determine which profiles are needed most to attain future performance goals.

Leadership Development Experts

Following is a list of suggestions for leadership and talent development experts, executive coaches, diversity consultants, and educators to help end the glass ceiling:

- Understand that women and men all need individualized coaching with accurate assessments (as can be found in the comprehensive CDR Character Assessment, CDR Risk Assessment, and CDR Drivers & Rewards Assessment). This is a critical first step to ensure an accurate reading of inherent strengths, risks, and needs.
- Consider becoming certified in an appropriate in-depth assessment instrument that includes a risk assessment for derailment, if you are an executive coach or leadership development instructor.
- Create accurate individual learning and development plans after the assessment and review process.
- Design learning curricula that develops leaders and professionals based on a diverse competency model, not just a male-oriented *Moving Against* model.
- Include coaching and training modules that focus on "Women as Worriers" as well as addressing other key risks of your client leaders. For example, our firm provides "Risk Factor Webinars" so that once someone is coached for their own risk factors, they can gain additional insights and training tips through these custom learning modules.
- Serve as a champion to redesign succession planning systems and executive competency models.
- Own the fact that *you* are a key catalyst and learning resource for the changes that will bring down the glass ceiling.
- Serve as a facilitator, trainer, and communicator to disseminate the research solutions and changes throughout the organization.

Women's Interest Groups

Of course, women need to help women. Young and experienced employees need to provide support for one another. Therefore, I encourage women's organizations to

- Share the knowledge and research.
- Hold forums and conferences and share this data.
- Offer assessments for women to begin the coaching or
  training process.
- Offer training and coaching from coaches who use
  scientifically validated deep dive tools.
- Mentor and coach women on the upswing how to develop
  their true talent.
- Write, publish, and speak.
- Get creative.
- Help men to understand women's inherent risk factors and
  perception differences.
- Partner together to bring down the glass ceiling!

FIFTEEN

The Glass Ceiling Ends

*"My vision is that the glass ceiling will be
in the rearview mirror within a decade."*

—Nancy Parsons

Summary of Eight Practical Steps to End the Glass Ceiling

Executive, leadership, and diversity teams should explore how they can best design action plans to turn around the current practices and biases in their organizations. Here are eight steps you can implement in your organization:

1. **Use scientifically validated, objective assessments** that accurately measure personality characteristics and strengths, risk factors for derailment, and drivers and reward (motivational) needs. Use these tools to identify, develop, and coach, and as a key part of promotional and succession planning decisions.

2. **Leadership Development and Training.** Ideally, identify *authentic leader talent* strengths, risks, and motivational needs for each leader and potential leader. Develop leaders based on their inherent individual strengths, talents, gaps, risks, and needs. Generic models and "group think" are not effective.

3. **Design leadership development solutions that are customized to address the needs of all leaders based on their own unique profiles.** Many women will need development to manage and neutralize their Worrier traits more effectively. However, the key is to understand that cookie-cutter training or coaching is not suitable because all leaders have specific, individual needs. While this research shows the trends, there are men and women leaders and high-potential staff who don't fit these trends. If a woman is a Worrier and Detached, help her develop past these vulnerabilities. If a man is an Upstager and False Advocate, help him develop past these traits to be more effective. And so on.

4. **Design and deliver cultural change training** throughout the organization that demonstrates *how perceptions are often wrong and are more damaging to aspiring women.* Also, share the gender research findings reported in this book. *(Please respect CDR copyrights for this research. We are glad to make a slide deck of these materials available for your use by contacting order@cdrassessmentgroup.com).*

5. **Design strategic organization-wide development, communication, promotional decisions, succession planning, and selection processes** that *endorse the individual strengths and gifts of women and men.* Help them manage and neutralize their specific risk factors.

6. **Clarify that the Worrier risk trait for a woman should not be a career-ending or blocking characteristic**. Those with this risk factor can make improvements to be more assertive, to stay at the table, and to demonstrate improved confidence. They need to leverage their strengths to help them neutralize and overcome this tendency.

7. **Hold all leaders accountable** for "bad" or inappropriate behaviors. Acting as an intimidating bully or dominating airtime should not be a ticket to success any longer. Stop allowing male leaders to behave this way and stop judging women more harshly. Treating everyone with respect should be a standard way of doing business. Men or women who don't do this should not be promoted up the chain of command.

8. Traditional mentoring, training, women's groups, etc., are not making the necessary inroads to bring down the glass ceiling, although they are certainly helping women. While these initiatives need to continue and perhaps be escalated, *the personnel facilitating these programs also need to be keenly aware of the new research* and of their mentee's assessment results to incorporate into their developmental processes for women.

The Power of Women to END the Glass Ceiling

What is so exciting and invigorating is that women have the capacity to end the glass ceiling. Most women are, indeed, Worriers. The key is identifying this risk, taking ownership, and doing something about it. We don't need to freeze in fear or be handicapped. By gaining a deep sense of self-awareness of strengths, risks, and needs, women can manage, prevent, and neutralize their risks so they do not derail their success and upward trajectory. It will take determination. It will take conscious effort. Women are up to the challenge. We have the power to end the glass ceiling.

Clearly, billions of dollars are being invested in women-in-leadership initiatives and most organizations. We just need to shift the resources to design and deploy in ways to support women, as individuals, based on their true talent and risk factors. No more scanning the surface or one-size-fits all training.

Organizations need to begin holding men and women both accountable for their risk behaviors. These ineffective coping behaviors are not productive and undermine success. No more looking the other way and promoting men while ignoring their risk behaviors.

It is time to begin using selection and succession planning procedures that objectively screen in highly talented diverse leaders. Adding scientifically validated assessments to talent management processes to identify true high potential talent is essential.

No more walking on eggshells for men and women leaders. Let's build trusting and respectful relationships and hold leaders with bad behaviors accountable. Let's communicate, build positive relationships, and perform as effective teams and team members, regardless gender (or other differences.)

Women do have the power. Women are amazingly gifted, driven, and talented as leaders. Women no longer need to allow their fear or need for perfection to derail their upward success. Women have the power to face their Worrier risk, analyze it, conquer, and manage it. Women leaders are strong and have exceptional capability, they just need to tackle and beat this one last obstacle in their way, the Worrier risk.

Vision 2030: The Glass Ceiling Ends

As the glass ceiling melts away, leadership performance success naturally increases. No longer will we have to live with 50% – 75% leadership ineffectiveness. Perhaps by the year 2030, we will decrease ineffective performance to 20% or less. Imagine the revenue! Imagine the innovation! Imagine the competitive advantage! Imagine the positive teams and work cultures emerging in organizations! Imagine finding, developing, and promoting those women and men leaders with true talent! Imagine where there is no more "club membership," wrongheaded perceptions, or biases leading the way! I see that world. I see it in a decade. Do you?

Looking Forward

With women using their power and being supported by stakeholders, I envision the glass ceiling will

- Begin to disappear in the early 2020s and will be gone by late 2030
- No longer hinder women's upward leadership success
- Not be a mystery but instead a problem largely solved by identifying the root cause, making the solutions clear
- No longer cost organizations billions of dollars a year in lost opportunities
- Stop hindering leadership performance, with effectiveness rates soaring
- Come down—swiftly! Of course, in a win-win productive and positive way for all

Let's get started.

SIXTEEN

The Research Findings

"Leadership and learning are
indispensable to each other."

—*John F. Kennedy*

In this chapter, you will find the results of each part of our personality-based leader study and graphed results that have been referred to throughout the book.

Illustration 8 shows the averaged CDR Risk Assessment results of our initial study of a random selection of male and female leaders across 35 organizations. In examining the data, women have statistically significant Worrier scores—more than five percentage points higher—while men have statistically higher scores in Egotist, Rule Breaker, and Upstager.

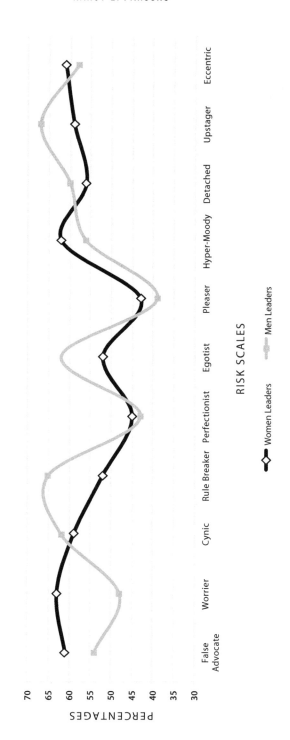

ILLUSTRATION 8
CDR Risk Assessment Average Scores ▪ Original Study Group

Reviewing the Profiles of Corporate Executive Women and Women CEOs

We began the next phase of our research to determine whether women in mid-level leadership's risk factors were different from women executives. We created study groups of successful women from five different EWF International Executive Peer Coaching groups from Oklahoma and Texas. We studied 22 female CEOs and 28 female corporate executives. No doubt, these women had immense determination, resolve, and talent. So many women do! Our research showed that there is a marked difference between the women in our first study group who were held back by the glass ceiling and the women in the later study group who are CEOs and other corporate executives.

Differences in Original Study Group vs. CEOs and Corp. Executives

Illustration 9 provides the group averages of all of the four groups in the original study across all of the CDR Risk Assessment scales. This shows the general trends and differences from group to group.

ILLUSTRATION 9

CDR Risk Assessment Average Scores -
Differences in Original Study Group vs. CEOs & Corp. Executives

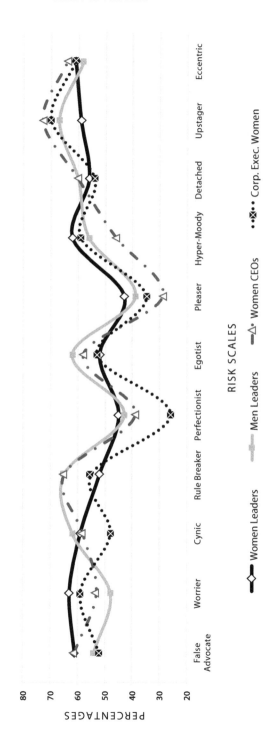

How Female CEOs and Corporate Executive Women Differed from the Women in the First Study Group

First, and most importantly, both the female CEO and corporate executive women groups had higher Upstager scores. They tell, sell, become pushy, persuade, and negotiate to get their way without backing down. As you will recall, the male leader group shared the high Upstager risk factor. Like the men, executive women and female CEOs stay at the table and engage during conflict and adversity. They do not retreat in fear like women stuck beneath the glass ceiling often do. Next, the female CEOs' scores are nearly identical to the male leader study group's scores when comparing their CDR Risk Factors.

The Female CEOs Are Egotists, Upstagers, and Rule Breakers

When facing adversity, conflict, and tough challenges, the female CEOs go into aggressive mode—and are willing to step up and fight and prevail. In addition, these women scored high as Rule Breakers, Upstagers, and Egotists—similar to the male leader group—so they will impulsively turn to aggression, go around bureaucracies, and ignore a policy or two to achieve their goals. They will also be pushy, appear courageous, and be bold in their assertions. Most of the CEOs studied were entrepreneurs.

Illustration 10 only shows the four key CDR Risks compared by study group. Notice how the female CEOs and male leaders' risks align and how those who tend to get past the glass ceiling all have high Upstager scores. Illustration 10 is an excerpt from Illustration 9 of the key scales impacting the glass ceiling. The arrows and circles are to point out key scoring averages where differences are found.

ILLUSTRATION 10

CDR Risk Assessment Average Scores: A Closer Look

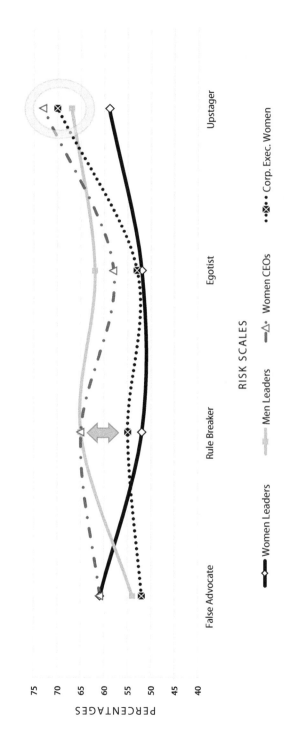

New 2018 Study Group: Western European Study (Source: IE Business School Results)

The gender-based findings of the CDR Risk Assessment for the IE Business School leaders and executives include 438 participants: 145 women leaders, of which 6 were executive women. There were 264 men leaders and 29 executive men in this study for a total of 293 men. While the sample size of the executive women was small (N=6), we viewed it as a trend and compared it to trends of executive/CEO women in our original North American studies.

In the following Illustration 11, the AMP (Advanced Management Program) women and men are those who are in mid-level leadership roles. The SMP (Senior Management Program) women and men are those who are in executive posts in the Western European study. In other words, SMP women have made it past the glass ceiling.

ILLUSTRATION 11

**Leader Group Risk Comparison, Western European Study
(Source: IE Business School)**

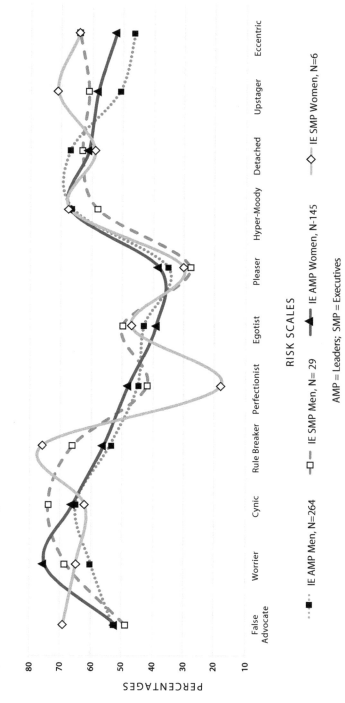

ILLUSTRATION 12

CDR Risk Assessment: Averaged Scores of Study Groups

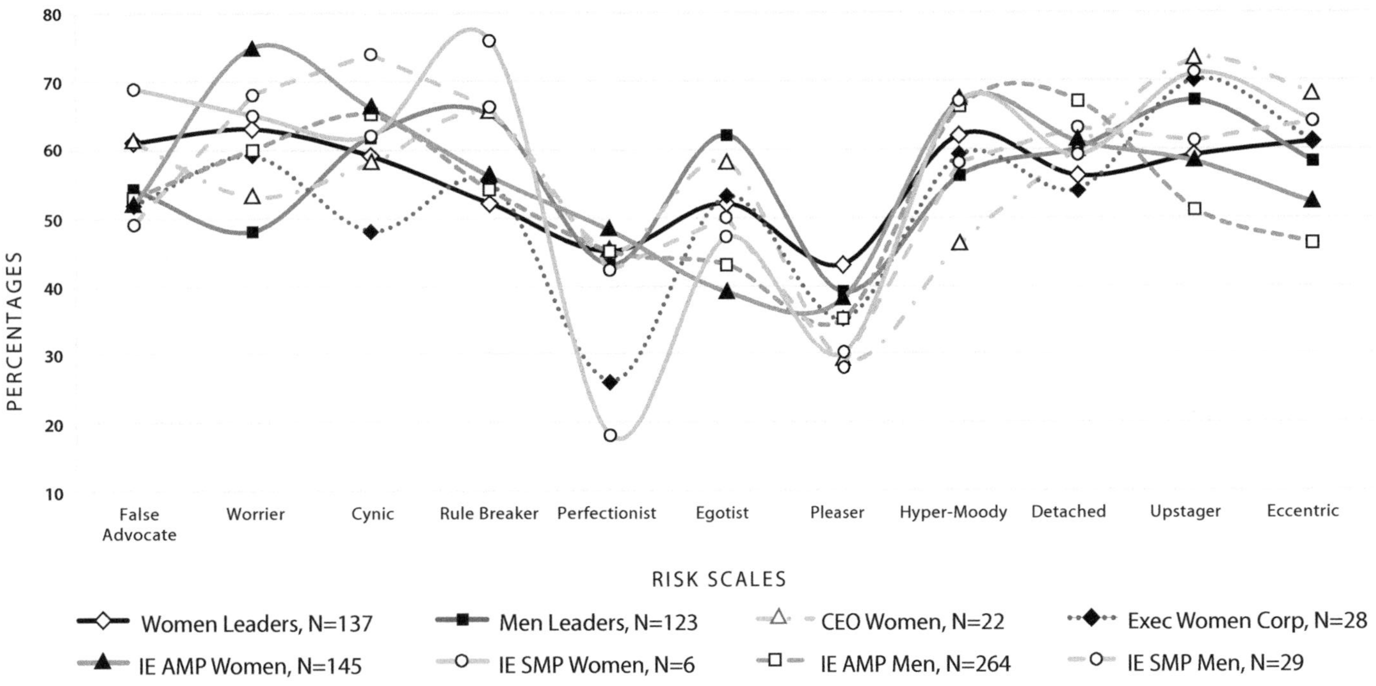

PERCENTAGES

RISK SCALES

False Advocate · Worrier · Cynic · Rule Breaker · Perfectionist · Egotist · Pleaser · Hyper-Moody · Detached · Upstager · Eccentric

◇— Women Leaders, N=137
▲— IE AMP Women, N=145
■— Men Leaders, N=123
○— IE SMP Women, N=6
△— CEO Women, N=22
□— IE AMP Men, N=264
◆— Exec Women Corp, N=28
○— IE SMP Men, N=29

This Illustration shows the average scores of all leader and executive groups by gender for North America and Western Europe.

Next, Illustration 13 shows only the Western Europe (IE) group results. Again, the men in the study group's risk trends do not match those of the North America men in the study. While the women leaders tended to be the highest Worriers at 75% overall, the men leaders were also Worriers, Detached, and Hyper-Moody. Both of these leader groups have *Moving Away* risk profiles. The executive women's group (SMP), albeit not a large enough sample in size at 6, who showed *Moving Against* risk traits also had significantly higher scores in Rule Breaker and Upstager. They, too, had an elevation in Worrier and Hyper-Moody. Lastly, the Western European men executives' highest risk was Cynic, which is a *Moving Away* risk factor. Their next highest trends were Rule Breaker, Worrier, Eccentric, Detached, and Upstager. These executive men had a mix of both *Moving Away* and *Moving Against* risk trends.

Illustration 13 takes a closer look at the key highest scales of each respective group, so not all risk scales are shown.

ILLUSTRATION 13

CDR Risk Assessment: Western Europe (IE)
Group Results of Significant Risk Trends

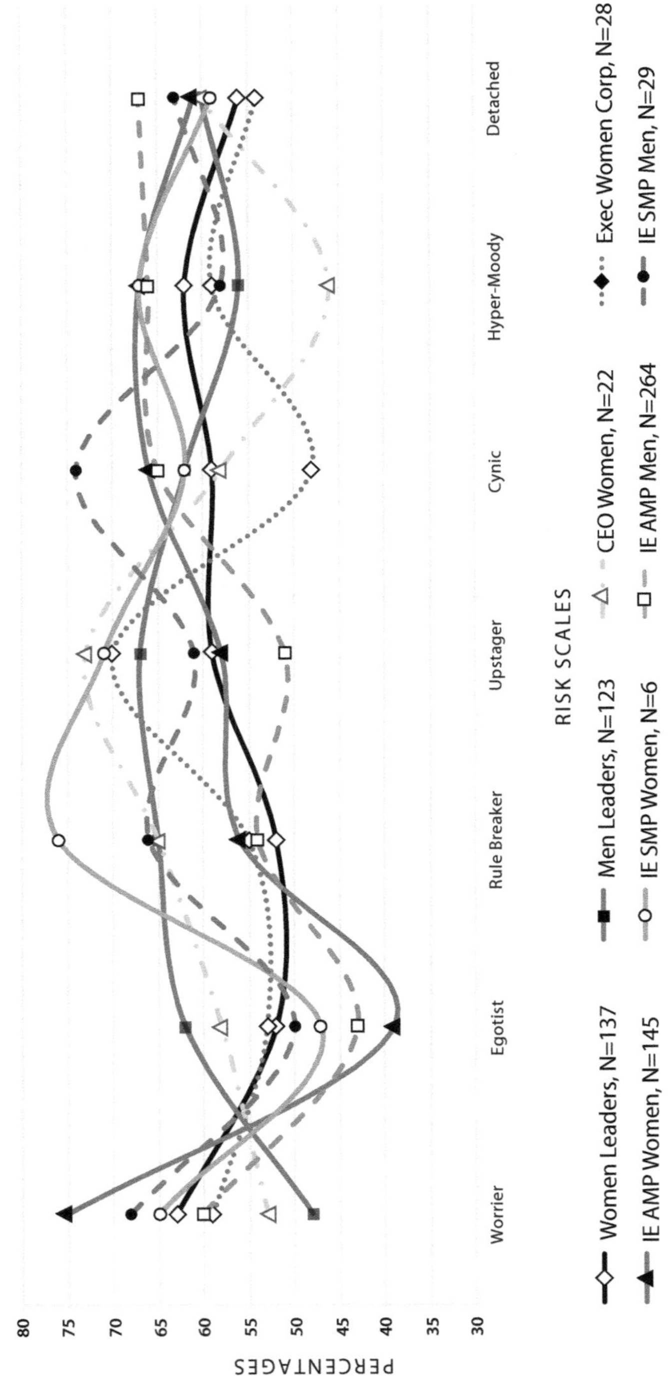

More research is needed into the Western European men's risks, impact of biases, and performance variables.

The bottom line is that in the US and Europe, *women hold less than 7% of the CEO positions*. and women leaders' (non-executives), who should be in the succession planning pipeline in both North America and Western Europe, highest risk factor is as Worriers.

Summaries of Each Leader Group

Northern America Men Leaders' Key Risks – EGOTIST, RULE BREAKER, and UPSTAGER

Men *Move Against*, fight for resources, fight for airtime, and aggressively win the day, albeit with over-the-top, excessively assertive, and "brave" tendencies. They are Egotists, Rule Breakers, and Upstagers. Men win the perception battle by having the stamina to stay in the game and fight to the end. During conflict or adverse situations, men leaders will do what it takes to succeed, even if it defies the rules or even behavioral standards for leaders.

North America Women Leaders and IE.edu Women Leaders Key Risk Different – THE WORRIER FACTOR

Women leaders fall in line with the Worrier mode and are afraid of failure and making a mistake. They study, analyze, and restudy under conflict or adversity. Their fearful and cautious approach involving *Moving Away* from conflict results in women being judged as lacking courage and confidence. This is why women are disproportionately bypassed for promotions—i.e., a key reason why the glass ceiling stays strong.

Women CEO Group Key Risks (with similarities to the IE SMP Women) – UPSTAGERS, RULE BREAKERS, and EGOTISTS

CEOs and SMP executive women's risk profiles are more similar to the North American men leader group than the women's. They are Upstagers, Rule Breakers, and Egotists. Therefore, even during conflict or difficult situations, they fight for resources, speak their minds, and will go against the grain or convention to succeed.

Women Corporate Executives – UPSTAGERS

Corporate executive women share a mixed risk profile. They share high Upstager with the men's leader group and the CEO women's group. They have a moderately high Worrier score, although it is their high Upstager that helps them stay engaged and asserting themselves even during tough discussions. In CDR's research, corporate executive women had very high Interpersonal Sensitivity scores on the CDR Character Assessment, which provides them with great relationship-building and networking skills to help them succeed. The good news for leadership effectiveness is that these corporate executive women's groups, unlike the men leaders and CEO women, have lower Egotist scores.

Western European Men Leaders –WORRIERS, DETACHED, CYNICS, and HYPER-MOODY

The Western European men's risks were different from the original study of North American men leaders. Western European men leaders are Worriers, Detached, Cynics, and Hyper-Moody. This means that they have *Moving Away* risk profiles and are conflict avoidant under stress for the most part. The Cynic risk is a *Moving Against* risk, a tendency to doubt others or over question new ideas. With the Worrier as their highest risk, although not as high as the women's IE group, they will also be rather risk aversive, slow decision makers, and be prone to overanalyzing situations. Their Hyper-Moody risk factor can trigger emotional responses including their Detachment, and the need to go quiet and isolate. So, they back away, go inside their heads, doubt others, and avoid confrontations.

Lastly, the highest risk for the Western European men executives group was Cynic, which is a *Moving Away* risk factor. Their next highest trends were Rule Breaker, Worrier, Eccentric, Detached, and Upstager. These executive men have a mix of both *Moving Away* and *Moving Against* risk trends.

Corporate Executive Women's Relationship-Building Skills – A KEY TO THEIR SUCCESS!

One other notable trend for the corporate executive women group is that their Interpersonal Sensitivity scores on the CDR Character Assessment [61] were significantly higher than all other groups, as seen in Illustration 14 below. This means that the corporate executive women are very skilled at building and maintaining effective relationships. This helps them to navigate to higher levels and win the perception battles. This also helps them succeed and thrive within the political structures of the organization. They are also better at building effective teams, networking, serving as talent coaches and mentors, and honing in on the needs and concerns of their stakeholders, including direct reports.

Illustration 14 shows the CDR Character Assessment average scores from the original North America Study of men and women at different leadership positions.

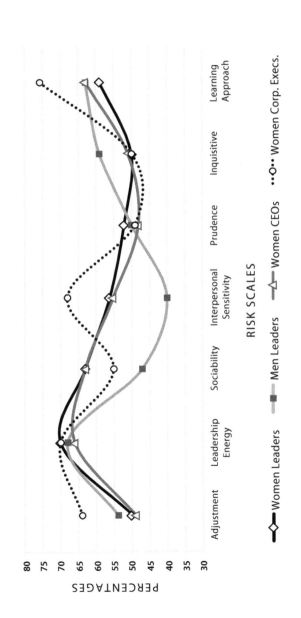

ILLUSTRATION 14
CDR Character Assessment Average Scores

Notice on Illustration 15 below from the IE.edu Western European shows similar strengths for women in that they are all (both groups) stronger at relationship building and networking due to their higher Interpersonal Sensitivity. This also indicates that the Western European men tend to be more strategic than operational and the women are the opposite. This is shown by the statistically significant higher scores in Inquisitive of the men whereas the women tend to have higher Prudence or operational focus.

ILLUSTRATION 15
Western European CDR Character Assessment Averaged Scores

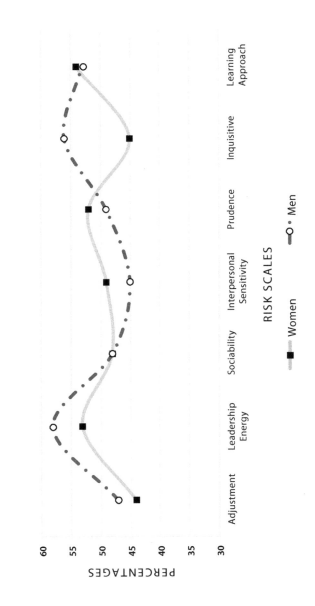

RISK SCALES

■ Women   ⊙ Men

n=151 women, n=294 men

See the following definition from the CDR Character Assessment report for Interpersonal Sensitivity, the key scale difference demonstrated in Illustration 15:

> *Interpersonal Sensitivity* measures the extent to which a leader is warm, caring, and sensitive towards the needs of others, is interpersonally skilled and perceptive versus being task-focused, hard-nosed, and apathetic toward the needs of others. Subscales for Interpersonal Sensitivity include cooperativeness, supportiveness, compassion, enjoyment of others, and lack of hostility.

A full listing of the CDR Character scales can be found in Chapter 5. Additional details about the research findings can be found in Chapter 5 with themes of findings being the focus of the book. Information about research methodology is covered in Appendix I.

APPENDIX I

Recommended Resources to Help Manage Leadership Risk Factors

Recommended Reading

There are many books, articles, podcasts, organizations, and tools to help women (and men) become more effective leaders, coaches, and mentors. Here is a list of some of our favorite, most of which focus on the risks and challenges noted in this book.

For Worriers:

> Brown, Brené, *Dare to Lead: Brave Work. Tough Conversations. Whole Hearts.* (New York: Random House, 2018).
>
> Duckworth, Angela, *GRIT–The Power of Passion and Perseverance* (New York: Scribner, 2016).
>
> Eblin, Scott, *Overworked and Overwhelmed* (Hoboken: Wiley & Sons, 2014).
>
> Helgesen, Sally and Marshall Goldsmith, *How Women Rise: Break the 12 Habits Holding You Back from Your Next Raise, Promotion, or Job*, (New York: Hachette Book Group, 2018).
>
> Hollis, Rachel, Girl, *Stop Apologizing: A Shame-Free Plan for Embracing and Achieving Your Goals* (N.p.: HarperCollins Leadership, 2019).
>
> Mohr, Tara, *Playing Big: Find Your Voice, Your Mission, Your Message* (New York: Penguin Books, 2014).
>
> Obuchowchowski, Pat, *Gutsy Women Win*, (Austin: River Grove Books, 2017).
>
> Shames, Deborah, *Out Front: How Women Can Become Engaging, Memorable, and Fearless Speakers* (Dallas: BenBella Books, 2017).
>
> White, Kate, *The Gutsy Girl Handbook: Your Manifesto for Success* (New York: Hachette Book Group, 2018).

For Egotists:

> Grant, Adam, *Give and Take: Why Helping Others Drives Our Success* (New York: Penguin Books, 2014).
>
> Holiday, Ryan, *Ego is the Enemy* (New York: Penguin Books, 2016).

Maccoby, Michael, *Narcissistic Leaders: Who Succeeds and Who Fails* (N.p.: Harvard Business Review Press, 2007).

Sinek, Simon, *Leaders Eat Last: Why Some Teams Pull Together and Others Don't*, Revised ed. (New York: Penguin Books, 2017).

For Rule Breakers:

Hurley, Robert, *The Decision to Trust: How Leaders Create High-Trust Organizations* (San Francisco: Jossey-Bass, 2011).

Lennick, Doug and Fred Kiel, *Moral Intelligence 2.0: Enhancing Business Performance and Leadership Success in Turbulent Times* (Boston: Pearson Education, 2011).

Pearson, Christine and Christine Porath, *The Cost of Bad Behavior: How Incivility Is Damaging Your Business and What to Do About It* (New York: Penguin Books, 2009).

Smith Meeks, Janet, *Gracious Leadership* (N.p.: Smart Business Books, 2018).

For Upstagers:

Bradberry, Travis, and Jean Greaves, *Emotional Intelligence 2.0.* (San Diego: TalentSmart, 2009).

Goulston, Mark, *Just Listen: Discover the Secret to Getting Through to Absolutely Anyone* (New York: AMACOM, 2009).

Patterson, Kelly, Joseph Grenny, Ron McMillan, and Al Switzler, *Crucial Conversations: Tools for Talking When Stakes Are High*, 2nd ed. (New York: McGraw-Hill Education, 2011).

Tumlin, Geoffrey, *Stop Talking, Start Communicating: Counterintuitive Secrets to Success in Business and in Life* (New York: McGraw-Hill Education, 2013).

On Executive Presence:

Garfinkle, Joel, *Executive Presence*, available at https://garfinkleexecutivecoaching.com/books/executive-presence

Hewlett, Sylvia Ann, *Executive Presence: The Missing Link Between Merit and Success* (New York.: HarperBusiness, 2014).

Salafafia, Rob, *Leading from Your Best Self: Develop Executive Poise, Presence, and Influence to Maximize Your Potential* (New York: McGraw Hill, 2018).

Must-Reads for All Leaders:

Hagemann, Bonnie, Simon Vetter, and John Marketa, *Leading with Vision* (London: Nicholas Brealey Publishing, 2017).

Kouzes, James and Barry Posner, *The Leadership Challenge*, 6th Ed. (San Francisco: Jossey-Bass, 2017).

Lencioni, Patrick, *The Advantage* (San Francisco: Jossey-Bass, 2012).

Scott, Kim, *Radical Candor* (New York: St. Martin's Press, 2017).

Oldies but Goodies:

Collins, Jim, *Good to Great: Why Some Companies Make the Leap and Others Don't* (New York: HarperCollins, 2001).

Kouzes, James and Barry Posner, *Credibility: Why Leaders Gain and Lose It, Why People Demand It* (San Francisco: Jossey-Bass, 1993).

Stowell, Steven J. and Matt, M. Starcevich, *The Coach* (N.p.: The Center for Management and Organizational Effectiveness, 1987). *(This book provides a practical 8 step model for leadership coaching. It turns this often messy engagement into a step-by-step process that works.)*

Articles by Nancy Parsons on Risk Factors and Drivers and Rewards:

Here are select articles or blog posts that can be found at www.cdrassessmentgroup.com/publications:

ARTICLE TITLE	RISK IMPACTED
Can You Train "Arrogance" Out of the Organization?	Egotist
Parallels Between "Extreme Narcissism" and the "Egotist" Leader	Egotist
Are You a "Rule Breaker?"	Rule Breaker
Six Leader Profiles That Reject Feedback	Egotist, Rule Breaker, Worrier
Improving Your Leader Voice • 8 Nuances of an Effective Leader Voice • Action Plans to Improve Your Leader Voice	All Risks That Undermine Communications, Particularly Upstager
Five Faces of A False Advocate	False Advocate
Developmental Insights for Pleasers	Pleasers
Do These 8 Bad Bosses Look Familiar?	Various Risks
Shining the Light on Passive-Aggressive Behaviors at Work	False Advocate
A Tip for Worriers	Worriers
The ODD Leadership Risk Factor that Can Derail Success	Eccentric
Are Any of the Eight Universal Derailers Undermining Your Success?	All Risks

Articles and Blog Posts About Drivers and Rewards Needs:

ARTICLE TITLE	RISK IMPACTED
What If—Love Was in the Air Every Day at Work?	All Drivers
Do You Have a Funny Bone?	Amusement & Hedonism (high & low scores)
Can a Leader Give Too Much Praise	All Drivers
The Artist that Hides Within	Artistic Endeavors
Rewards, Incentives & Gift Ideas for the Scientifically Driven Person	Scientific Reasoning

APPENDIX II

—◡—

Research
Methodology

Research

The research in this book essentially involved three steps:

1. Comparing inherent personality risk assessment results of mid-level men and women leader study groups to determine if there were any notable gender differences.
2. Analyzing personality, character, and risk assessment results compared to Pew Cultural Survey Results of the perceptions of men and women leaders.
3. Comparing the personality data (character and risks) of the first study groups to the data of the second study group of corporate executive women and CEO/entrepreneurial women's groups.

The Study Participants

In the first study that is shared in Chapter 5, we reviewed the CDR Risk Assessment results of mid-level leaders: 137 women and 122 men from 35 companies. In our second study, reported in Chapter 5, we analyzed the personality assessment results (character and risk assessments) of 30 corporate executive women and 21 women CEOs/entrepreneurs who were members of six different EWF International groups. Leaders in both of our studies were from more than eighty companies.

CDR Personality Assessments Used in the Research

Personality assessment is useful for describing an individual's characteristics that may not be directly observed. Behaviors are visible to people, but the reasons behind them and the motivations for them are not observable. Psychological assessment results provide a vocabulary for describing propensities and a view of the "whys" behind the behaviors. This information, in turn, allows for more effective employee selection, succession planning, team building, and professional development. In our studies related to the glass ceiling, we used personality measure results from the CDR Risk Assessment and CDR Character Assessment.

Companies and Sectors of Participants in Study Groups

The leaders in our studies were from more than eighty companies. Below are samples of sectors the leaders represent.

- Banking/Finance
- Chemical
- Communications/Media
- Department of Defense
- Education/Academia
- Energy
- Entertainment
- Federal Government
- Food Industries
- Healthcare
- Insurance
- Logistics
- Manufacturing
- Marketing/Advertising
- Medical Device
- Pharmaceutical
- Publishing
- Real Estate
- Retail
- Service/Consulting
- Transportation
- Utilities

Women's Organizations and Participation

EWF International provided us with participant access to obtain the data for our second study. EWF International was formed in 1998 and has created and facilitated peer advisory forum groups for women business owners and executives.[62] We worked with EWF's CEO and corporate executive women's peer executive groups. We worked with a total of six groups that were based in Tulsa, Oklahoma City, and Dallas, Texas.

We also facilitated workshops for these women's forums, during which we reviewed our research results and provided group leadership training. In addition, we held workshops to debrief the character, risks, and in some cases, CDR Drivers & Rewards Assessment results with all of the participating female executives. Many of these executive women also opted to go through one-on-one coaching with their CDR 3-D Suite results.

For more than four years, IE Business School in Madrid, Spain, has incorporated the CDR 3-D Suite and executive coaching into their executive education programs and select MBA programs. In late 2018, we completed a third study of 438 Western European participants who were women leaders, women executives, men executives, and men leaders, and the results were even more stark for women leaders. This data was compiled from IE Business School program participants from their Executive Education department, which included women leaders, men leaders, and executives. The women leader group's sample size was slightly larger, with 145 women, and the men leader group's sample size was 264, with 29 being men in executive roles. The sample size for the executive women's group in Western Europe (IE.edu) was not large enough, with only six participants.

Pew Cultural Survey

The Pew Cultural Survey Report that summarized key trends over time in the movement of women into leadership positions in politics, business, the labor force, and the professions was used in this book. In Chapter 6, we introduced the cultural bias of men versus women and then compared the Pew Survey results to CDR Personality Character and Risk Assessment results.

CDR Assessment Validity Process

When developing a personality assessment, the first question to answer is what to measure. Items are then written to reflect the behaviors associated with the dimension(s) being measured. For example, extroversion is defined as "interest in or behavior directed toward others." Thus, items to measure extroversion might be written to indicate the degree to which a person enjoys (or does not enjoy) social settings, crowded events, and making presentations. Sample items focusing on extroversion might be: "In a group, I enjoy attracting attention to myself," or "I don't care for large, noisy crowds."

Pool size is determined by the number of dimensions being assessed and the number of items deemed necessary to tap into each dimension. Once a pool of test items are written, the items are pilot tested to determine the degree to which they correlate with each other. They differentiate people (some endorse, some do not), and they are reliable. Reliability is determined by test-retest (subjects answer the question the same way on multiple administrations) and by internal consistency (items which are designed to measure extroversion tend to correlate or hang together).

The next step is to determine the validity of the measure, which is a bit more complicated to explain. First, there is what's known as the test-test validation process, which correlates scores on our instruments with other instruments. These test-to-test correlations are conducted with instruments that are hypothesized to have similar or related constructs and with instruments that are hypothesized to be unrelated. For example, the process of validating a tool like the CDR Character Assessment includes having subjects take that instrument along with others such as the ASVAB, PSI Basic Skills Test, Myers-Briggs Type Indicator, Self-Directed Search (SDS), Interpersonal Adjective Scales, Big-Five Factor Markers Assessment, and the Minnesota Multiphasic Personality Inventory-2 (MMPI-2). These analyses result in correlations used to confirm hypothesized relationships.

The next level of validation included correlations between test scores and relevant non-test indicators, such as actual performance ratings. This step was taken to validate (confirm or not) whether the instrument accurately measures the predicted behavior and the impact on performance. For example, those who have high scores on the CDR Character Assessment Adjustment scale and a high CDR Risk Assessment Egotist score will generally have higher self-ratings on 360° performance reviews. This translates to people having higher opinions about their own performance in comparison with the perceptions of others. Thus, the correlations will be higher between these scale scores and the resulting behavior ratings. The validation process is not simple, and it is important to perform statistical analyses using a variety of non-test indicators and performance results. In addition to performance reviews, other examples of non-test indicators may include sales results, customer retention, customer complaints, accidents, turnover, errors, etc. When developed in 1998 for the CDR Character Assessment and the CDR Risk Assessment, we used an existing database with well-established norms and data that had over 300,000 and 100,000 cases, respectively.

About the Author

Nancy Parsons is one of today's foremost experts in combining the science of assessments with the art of developing people. She is the CEO/President of CDR Assessment Group, Inc. that she cofounded with Kimberly R. Leveridge, PhD. In 1998, together they authored the breakthrough CDR 3-Dimensional Assessment Suite® an ideal coaching tool which has been translated to five languages for global clients. The CDR 3-D Suite measures leadership character traits, inherent risk factors for derailment, and drivers and rewards.

Nancy provides executive coaching services for the C-Suite and leaders across all sectors, facilitates strategic executive team development sessions, and instructs "Authentic Leadership" workshops. She designed and continues to instruct the CDR Executive Coaches' Certification workshops and teaches advanced coaching and consulting programs for internal and external consultants. Nancy released her research-based book, *Fresh Insights to END the Glass Ceiling*, in 2017, has written more than 70 articles, and has published a blog since 2009. She has presented at international, national, and regional industry conferences. In 2019, she was designated as an International Thought Leader of Distinction in Executive Coaching by the MEECO Leadership Institute.

In addition to her professional activities, Parsons leads the philanthropic initiative Vets Coaching Vets, and is a member of both the

Alexcel Group and CoachSource global executive coaching organizations. She resides in Sugar Land, Texas with her husband and three very spoiled dogs.

To learn more about Nancy Parsons and CDR Assessment Group, Inc., visit www.cdrassessmentgroup.com.

About CDR Assessment Group, Inc.

Website: www.cdrassessmentgroup.com

LinkedIn: www.linkedin.com/company/cdr-assessment-group

Twitter: @CDR_Assessment and @NEParsons

We are a globally recognized assessment, leadership, and talent development firm leading the way with revolutionary products, executive coaching and consulting services, research, and training solutions. We are committed to providing cutting-edge leadership and talent development products and services to global clients, designed with the foremost psychological insights and applied business know-how.

Our Assessments

CDR 3-Dimensional Assessment Suite®

- CDR Character Assessment
- CDR Risk Assessment
- CDR Drivers & Rewards Assessment

Full interpretive developmental reports are available for each assessment to the subscale level. Reports are available in five languages. Additional reports include staffing/selection and interview questions.

360° Leader Scan™ is a multi-rater leadership performance and development instrument containing approximately eighty items, 10 core competency areas, and statistical and narrative input.

Executive Team Performance Forecast™, Strategic Team Analysis Surveys, Research, and several more custom products are available.

Our Services for Women in Leadership

1. Presentations on the topic of this book are available as a keynote speech, conference presentation, or executive/leadership workshop
2. Accelerated leadership coaching using the CDR 3-D Suite®
3. Women's Leadership Workshops
4. Coaches' Certification Workshops
5. Train the Trainer for Women's Leadership Workshops

Key Services

CDR-U – Talent Development

- Executive Coaching: We have a global team of CDR certified executive coaches available for client projects
- Authentic Leadership Programs
- Women in Leadership Workshops
- Strategic Team Development
- Executive Coaches' Certification and Advanced Coaches' Training
- Selection Screening Process Training
- Risk Factor Webinars
- CDR-U Online Learning

CDR-TM – Talent Management

- Leadership Capability Analysis
- Selection Screening
- Succession Planning
- Executive Team Performance Forecasts
- Interventions, Root Cause Analysis Projects
- Cultural and Incentive Studies
- Research Projects

Women's Leadership Workshop

Experts from CDR Assessment Group, Inc. and affiliated executive coaches offer this powerful and unmatched leadership development experience, exclusively for women. This is no ordinary or generic event. Women, if you are ready for a life-changing experience to zero in on your leadership strengths, emotional intelligence, personal needs, and risk factors, then this is a must-attend for you.

This development process will:

- Develop your approach to break through the glass ceiling
- Build your confidence to ask the tough questions
- Prepare you to deal with conflict more effectively
- Improve the balance between your professional and personal life
- Develop and sustain strategies for ongoing learning and growth

Women's Leadership Workshop includes:

1. Two-day custom workshop led by two expert instructors
2. CDR 3-D Suite®
3. One-to-one executive coaching (2.5 hours) prior to workshop and one post-workshop session
4. Personal branding, mission statement, and developmental action plan

Notes

1. Valentina Zarya, "The Share of Female CEOs in the Fortune 500 Dropped by 25% in 2018," *Fortune*, May 21, 2018, http://fortune.com/2018/05/21/women-fortune-500-2018.

2. "Pyramid: Women in S&P 500 Companies," *Catalyst*, accessed June 11, 2019, https://www.catalyst.org/knowledge/women-sp-500-companies.

3. Marcus Noland, Tyler Moran, and Barbara Kotschwar, "Is Gender Diversity Profitable? Evidence from a Global Survey," *Peterson Institute of Global Economics*, February 2019, https://piie.com/system/files/documents/wp16-3.pdf.

4. McKinsey & Company and LeanIn.Org, "Women in the Workplace 2018," *McKinsey & Company* and *LeanIn.Org*, 2018, https://womenintheworkplace.com.

5. "The Global Gender Gap Report 2018," *World Economic Forum*, 2018, http://www3.weforum.org/docs/WEF_GGGR_2018.pdf.

6. Valentina Zarya, "Since #MeToo, the Number of Men Who Are Uncomfortable Mentoring Women Has Tripled," *Fortune*, February 6, 2018, https://fortune.com/2018/02/06/lean-in-sheryl-sandberg.

7. Leah Fessler, "Sheryl Sandberg has a plan for the 50% of male managers afraid to mentor women," *Quartz at Work*, February 16, 2018, https://qz.com/work/1209389/facebook-coo-sheryl-sandberg-and-her-lean-in-nonprofit-wants-men-to-mentor-more-women/

8. McKinsey & Company and LeanIn.Org, "Women in the Workplace 2018."

9. Linda Napikoski, "How Women Became Part of the 1964 Civil Rights Act," *ThoughtCo*, February 15, 2019, https://www.thoughtco.com/women-and-the-civil-rights-act-3529477.

10. "Civil Rights Act of 1964," *History.com*, accessed September 20, 2018, https://www.history.com/topics/black-history/civil-rights-act.

11. "The Pregnancy Discrimination Act of 1978." US Equal Employment Opportunity Commission, accessed March 10, 2019, https://www.eeoc.gov/laws/statutes/pregnancy.cfm.

12. "Pyramid: Women in S&P 500 Companies."

13. John Bussey, "Women, Welch Clash at Forum," *The Wall Street Journal*, May 4, 2012, https://www.wsj.com/articles/SB10001424052702303877604577382321364803912?mg=id-wsj.

14. Rik Kirkland and Iris Bohnet, "Focusing on What Works for Workplace Diversity," *McKinsey & Company*, April 2017, www.mckinsey.com/featured-insights/gender-equality/focusing-on-what-works-for-workplace-diversity.

15. "Top Diversity Executive Salary in the United States," *Salary.com*, accessed March 10, 2019, https://www1.salary.com/Top-Diversity-Executive-Salary.html.

16. "BCG's Gender Diversity Research: By the Numbers," *BCG*, 2019, https://www.bcg.com/capabilities/diversity-inclusion/gender-diversity-research-by-numbers.aspx.

17. Frank Dobbin and Alexandra Kalev, "Why Diversity Programs Fail." *Harvard Business Review*, July/August 2016, https://hbr.org/2016/07/why-diversity-programs-fail.

18. Odette Chalaby, "Diversity Training Doesn't Change People's Behaviour. We Need to Find Out What Does." *World Economic Forum*, June 1, 2018, www.weforum.org/agenda/2018/06/diversity-training-change-behaviour-gender-equality-work.

19. Ibid.

20. Ibid.

21. McKinsey & Company and LeanIn.Org, "Women in the Workplace 2018."

22. James Damore, "Google's Ideological Echo Chamber: How Bias Clouds our Thinking About Diversity and Inclusion," July 2017, https://assets.documentcloud.org/documents/3914586/ Googles-Ideological-Echo-Chamber.pdf

23. Rick Wartzman, "Men Really Are Clueless About Their Female Coworkers," *Fortune*, March 10, 2016, www.fortune.com/2016/03/10/ men-really-are-clueless-about-women-at-work-glass-ceiling-pay-gap.

24. Romy Newman and Christy Johnson, "What Men Really Think About Gender in The Workplace," *Fairygodboss*, accessed March 10, 2019, https://fairygodboss.com/articles/ what-men-really-think-about-gender-in-the-workplace.

25. Matt Krentz, Olivier Wierzba, Katie Abiuzahr, Jennifer Garcias-Alonso, and Frances Brooks, "Five Ways Men Can Improve Gender Diversity at Work," *Boston Consulting Group*, October, 10, 2017, https://www.bcg.com/publications/2017/people-organization-behavior-culture-five-ways-men-improve-gender-diversity-work.aspx.

26. "Harvard IOP Spring 2016 Poll," *Harvard IOP*, April 25, 2016, http://iop.harvard.edu/youth-poll/harvard-iop-spring-2016-poll.

27. Nikki Graf, "Sexual Harassment at Work in the Era of #MeToo," *Pew Research Center*, April 4, 2018, www.pewsocialtrends.org/2018/04/04/ sexual-harassment-at-work-in-the-era-of-metoo.

28. Pragya Agarwal, "Here is Why We Need to Talk About Bullying in the Work Place," *Forbes*, July 29, 2018, www.forbes.com/sites/ pragyaagarwaleurope/2018/07/29/workplace-bullying-here-is-why-we-need-to-talk-about-bullying-in-the-work-place/#1ca90b93259a.

29. "Men and Women: No Big Difference," *American Psychological Association*, Oct. 20, 2005, https://www.apa.org/research/action/ difference.

30. Jack Zenger and Joseph Folkman, "Are Women Better Leaders than Men?," *Harvard Business Review*, Mar. 15, 2012, https://hbr.org/2012/03/a-study-in-leadership-women-do.

31. Linda-Eling Lee, Ric Marshall, Damion Rallis, and Moscardi, "Women on Boards." *MSCI Inc.*, November 2015, https://www.msci.com/documents/10199/04b6f646-d638-4878-9c61-4eb91748a82b.

32. Emily Chasan, "What Investors Get Wrong About Backing Women-Led Businesses," *Bloomberg*, December 27, 2018, https://www.bloomberg.com/news/articles/2018-12-27/what-investors-get-wrong-about-backing-women-led-businesses.

33. R. Kress, "Numbers Show Women-Led Companies Outperform Competitors," *Ivy Exec*, accessed March 10. 10, 2019, https://www.ivyexec.com/career-advice/2017/women-led-companies-outperform-competitors/#.

34. Janet Burns, "The Results Are In: Women Are Great For Business, But Still Getting Pushed Out," *Forbes*, September 22, 2017, https://www.forbes.com/sites/janetwburns/2017/09/22/2016-proved-women-are-great-for-business-yet-still-being-pushed-out/#3be07bb8188b.

35. Noland, Moran, and Kotschwar, "Is Gender Diversity Profitable? Evidence from a Global Survey."

36. John Scott, Allan Church, and Jillian McLellan, "Selecting Leadership Talent for the 21st-Century Workplace," *SHRM*, 2017, https://www.shrm.org/hr-today/trends-and-forecasting/special-reports-and-expert-views/Documents/Selecting-Leadership-Talent.pdf.

37. Leslie, Jean Britain, "The Leadership Gap: What You Need, and Still Don't Have, When It Comes to Leadership Talent," *Center for Creative Leadership*, accessed March 10, 2019, https://www.ccl.org/wp-content/uploads/2015/09/Leadership-Gap-What-You-Need.pdf.

38. Robert Kaiser and Gordy Curphy, "Leadership Development: The Failure of an Industry and the Opportunity for Consulting Psychologists," *Consulting Psychology Journal: Practice and Research* 2013, vol. 5, no 4 (2013): 294-302, http://doi.org/10.1037/a0035460.

39. Mark Crowley, "Gallup's Profound Discovery: Engagement Is Driven by Good Managers with Rare Talents," *Talent Culture*, September 19, 2017, https://talentculture.com/gallups-profound-discovery-engagement-is-driven-by-good-managers-with-rare-talents.

40. Erin Duffin, "Annual Corporate Profits in the US 2000-2017," *Statista*, accessed March 10, 2019, https://www.statista.com/statistics/222130/annual-corporate-profits-in-the-us.

41. Nancy Parsons, "Comparing Leadership Risk Factor Results to 360° Feedback," *CDR Assessment Group, Inc.*, Oct. 2015, http://cdrassessmentgroup.com/wp-content/uploads/2015/10CDR-Leader-Risks-and-360-Comparisons.pdf.

42. Juliana Horowitz, Ruth Igielnik, and Kim Parker, "Women in Leadership," *Pew Research Center*, September 20, 2018, http://www.pewsocialtrends.org/2018/09/20/women-and-leadership-2018.

43. "Men and Women: No Big Difference."

44. Sheryl Sandberg, *Lean In: Women, Work and the Will to Lead* (New York: Knopf Doubleday Publishing Group, 2013), 3.

45. Nancy Parsons and Kimberly Leveridge, *CDR Risk Assessment* (CDR Assessment Group, Inc., 1998).

46. Ibid.

47. Ibid.

48. Karen Horney, *Our Inner Conflicts: A Constructive Theory of Neurosis* (New York: W. W. Norton & Company, 1992), 14-16.

49. Jun Medalla, "7 Traits of Executive Presence, The Key to Winning People Over," *Business Insider*, September 24, 2013, https://www.businessinsider.com/the-7-traits-of-executive-presence-2013-9.

50. Natasha Gural, "How State Street Is Bypassing Recruiters To Attain Its Top Tier Hiring Targets," *eFinancialCareers*, July 9, 2013, http://news.efinancialcareers.com/us-en/145706/how-state-street-is-bypassing-recruiters-to-attain-its-top-tier-hiring-targets/.

51. Howard Ross, "Exploring Unconscious Bias," *Diversity Best Practices*, 2008, https://culturalawareness.com/wp-content/uploads/2017/03/Unconscious-Bias-White-Paper.pdf.

52. Juliana Horowitz, Ruth Igielnik, and Kim Parker, "Women in Leadership," *Pew Research Center*, September 20, 2018, http://www.pewsocialtrends.org/2018/09/20/women-and-leadership-2018.

53. Ibid.

54. Ibid.

55. Eric Jaffe, "The New Subtle Sexism Toward Women in the Workplace," *Fast Company*, June 2, 2014, https://www.fastcompany.com/3031101/the-new-subtle-sexism-toward-women-in-the-workplace.

56. *The New Soft War on Women: How the Myth of Female Ascendance Is Hurting Women, Men—and Our Economy*, Paperback – September 1, 2015

57. by Caryl Rivers (Author), Rosalind C. Barnett (Author)

58. Samantha Paustian-Underdahl, Lisa Slattery Walker, and David Woehr. "Perceptions of Leadership Effectiveness: A Meta-Analysis of Contextual Moderators," *Journal of Applied Psychology,* 99, no. 6 (2014): 1129-1145, http://www.doi.org/10.1037/a0036751.

59. Noland, Moran, and Kotschwar, "Is Gender Diversity Profitable? Evidence from a Global Survey."

60. Linda-Eling Lee, et al. "Women on Boards." *MSCI Inc.*, November 2015, https://www.msci.com/documents/10199/04b6f646-d638-4878-9c61-4eb91748a82b.

61. Noland, Moran, and Kotschwar, "Is Gender Diversity Profitable? Evidence from a Global Survey."

62. Nancy Parsons and Kimberly Leveridge, *CDR Character Assessment* (CDR Assessment Group, Inc., 1998).

63. Executive Women's Forum International (EWFI), accessed March 10, 2019, http://ewfinternational.com/about-ewf-international.